Doodling & Coloring Designs:

Mandalas

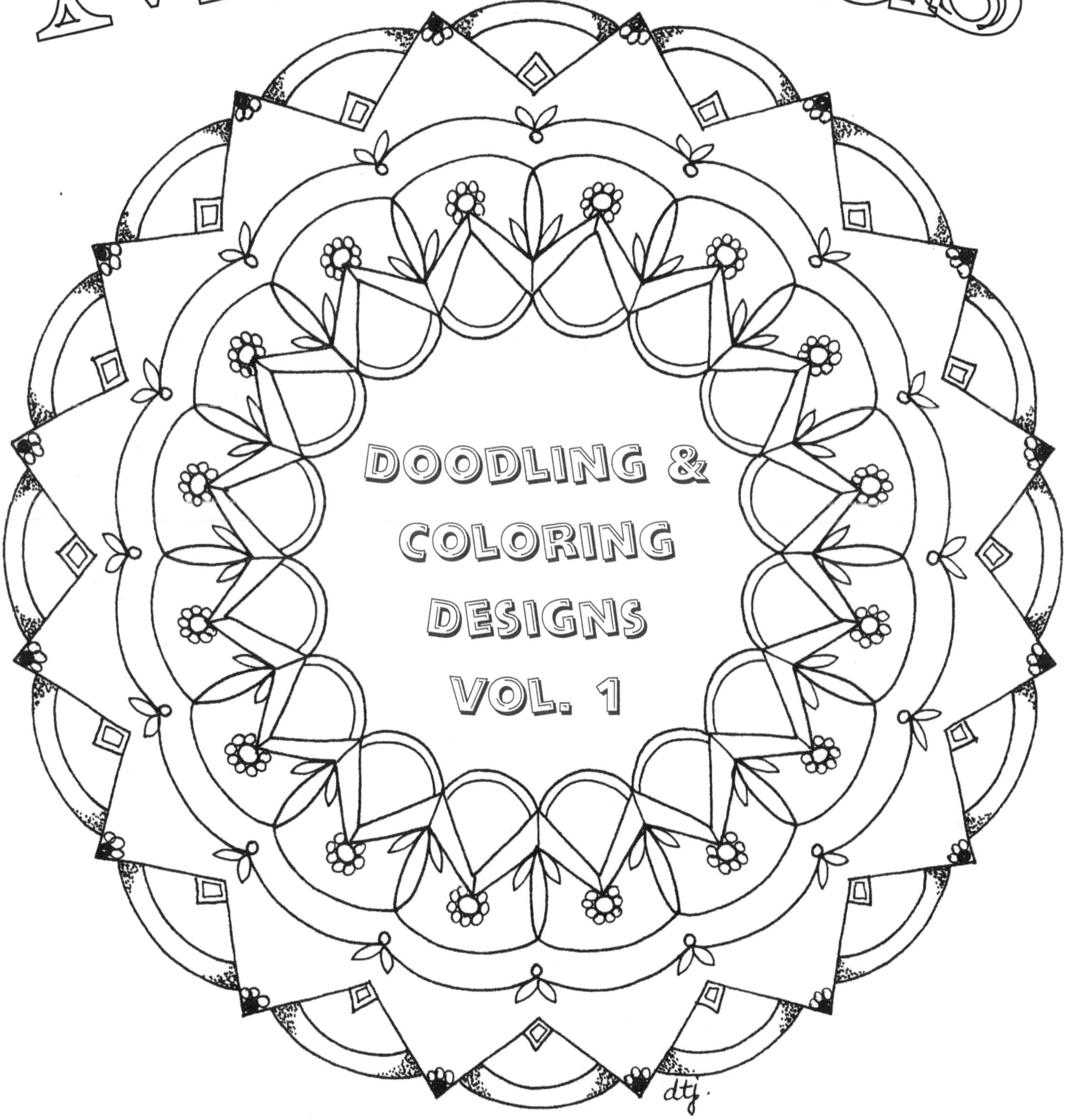

DOODLING &
COLORING
DESIGNS
VOL. 1

By Darla Sue Tjelmeland

Dedication

This coloring book is dedicated to:

My Facebook Group – *Doodling & Coloring Designs*. I wonderfully creative, inspirational and fun group of people who inspire and motivate me each and every day!

Author's note: I highly recommend that you place a sheet of card stock behind the page that you are coloring to prevent bleed-through of markers or gel pens on to the next coloring page.

Printed by CreateSpace, An Amazon.com Company

ISBN-13: 978-1519161208
ISBN-10: 1519161204

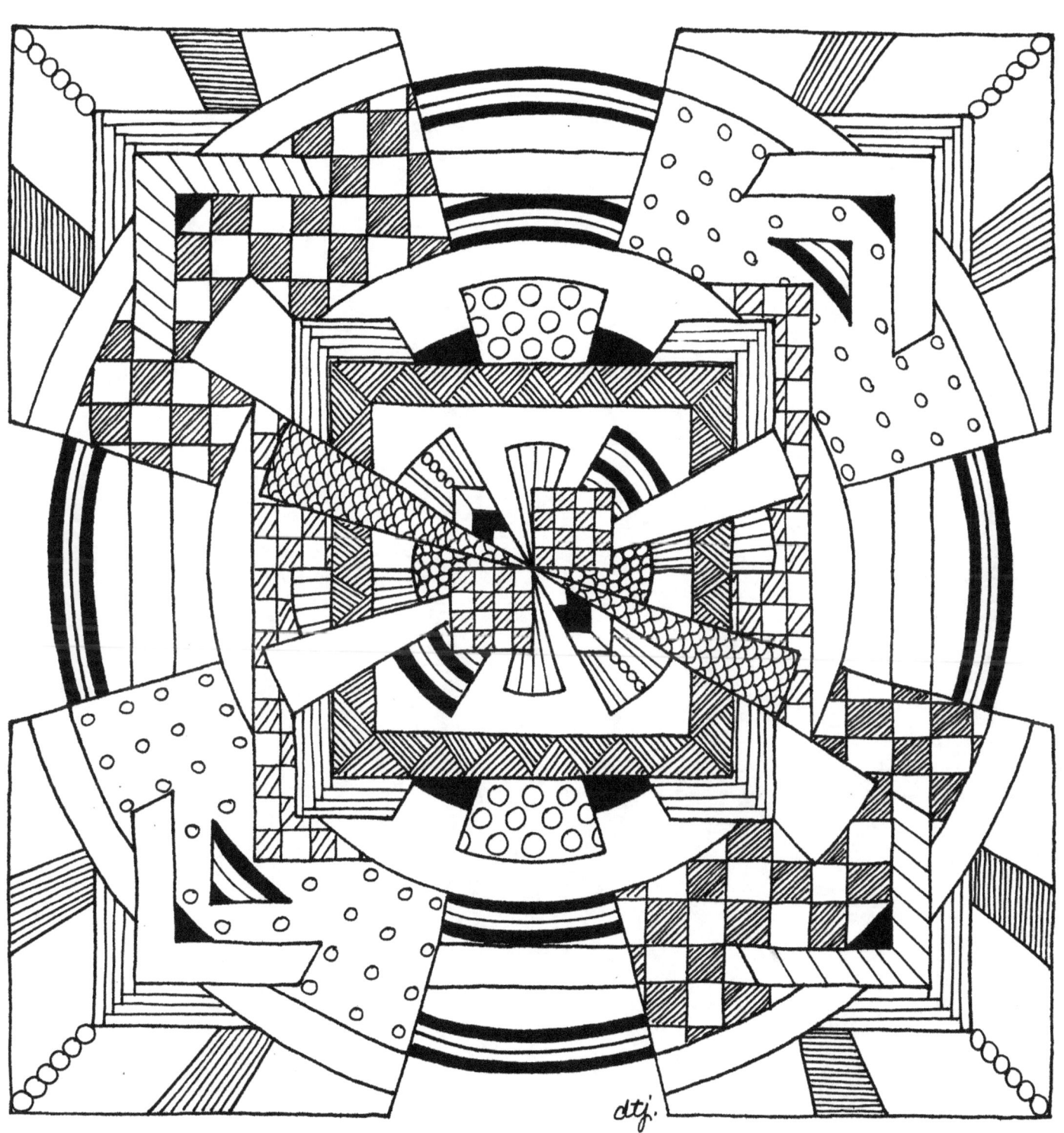

dtj.

Title: _____

Date: _____

Colorist: _____

_____

_____

_____

_____

_____

_____

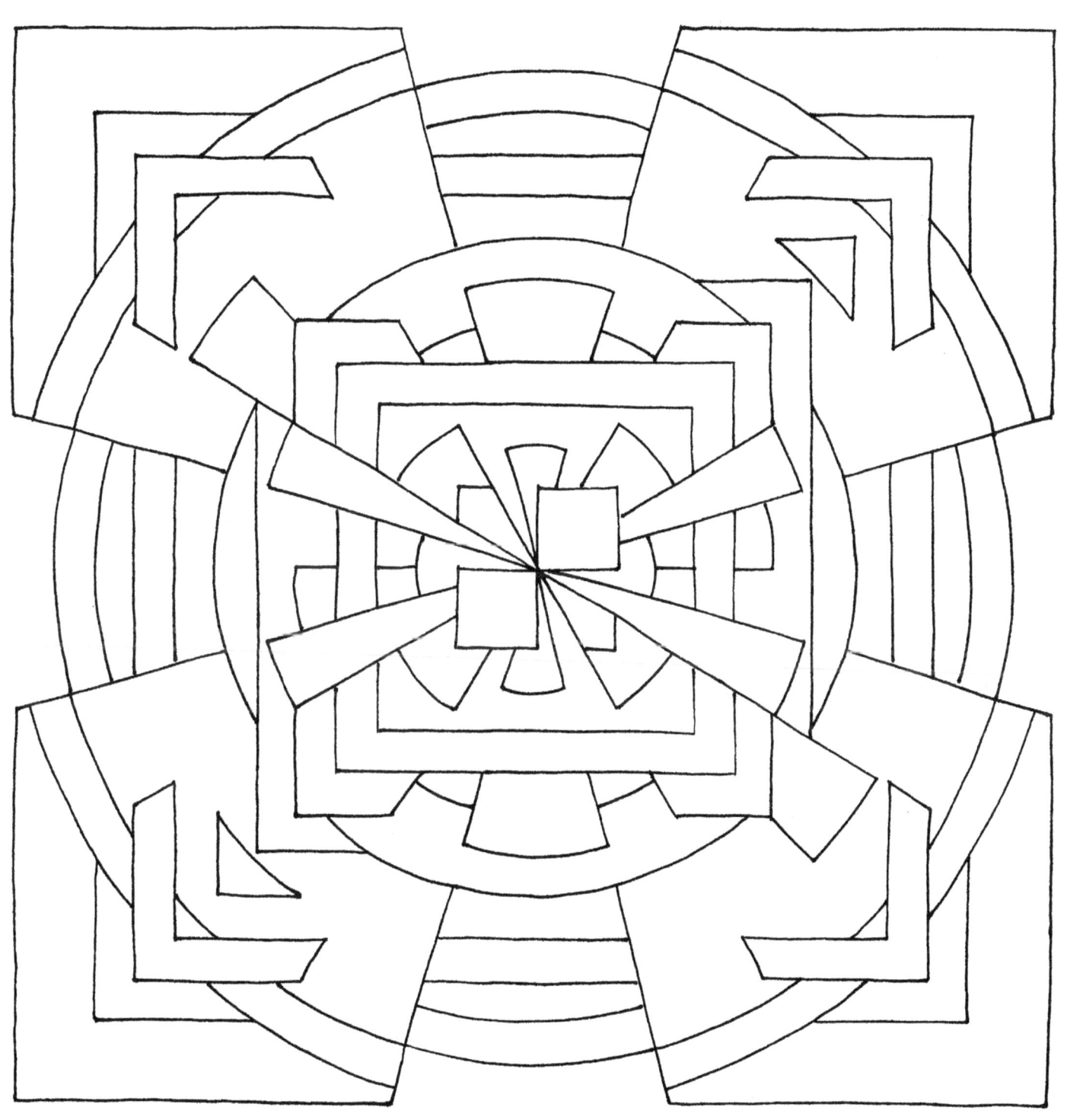

Title:

Date:

Artist:

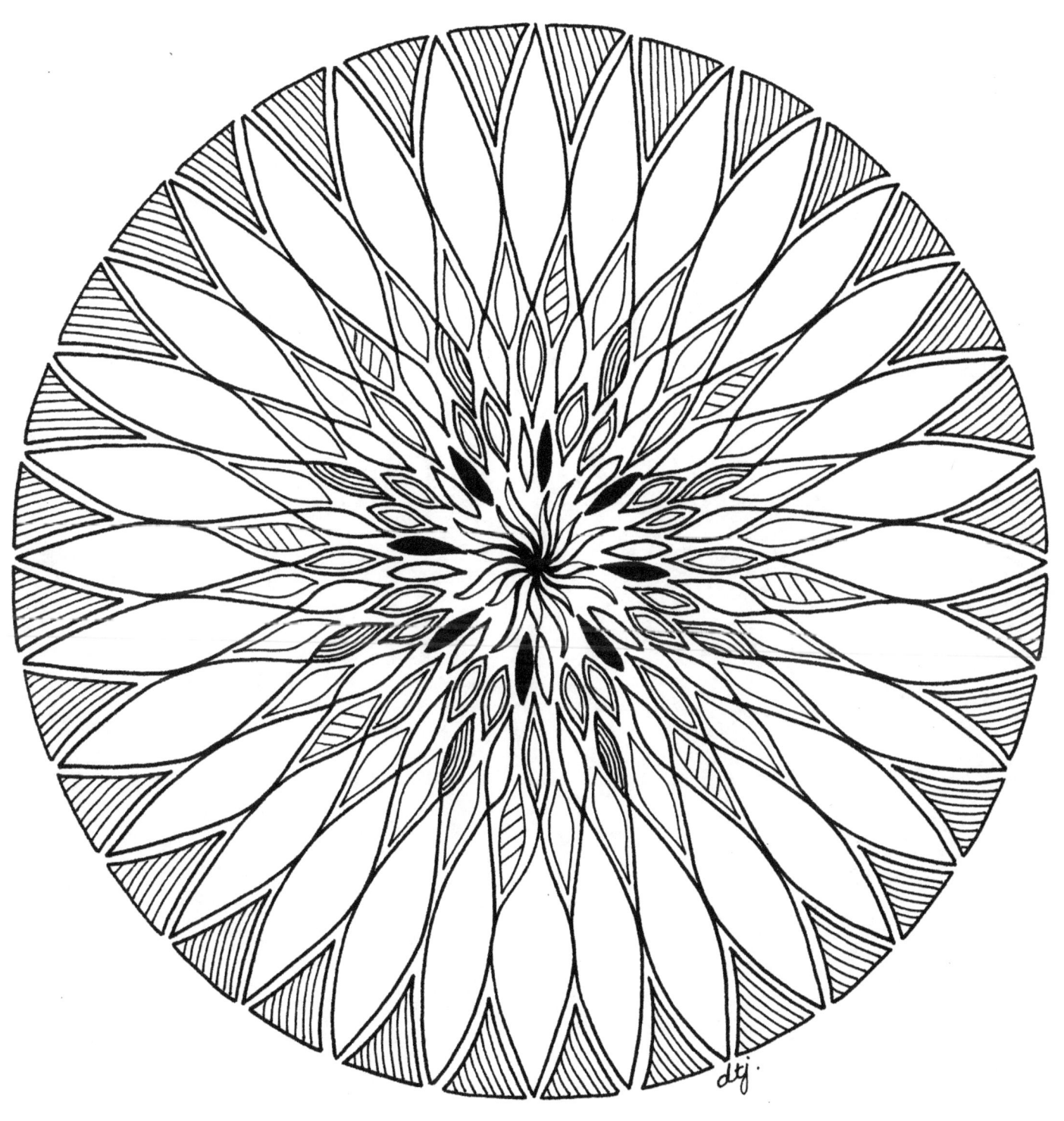

Title:

Date:

Colorist:

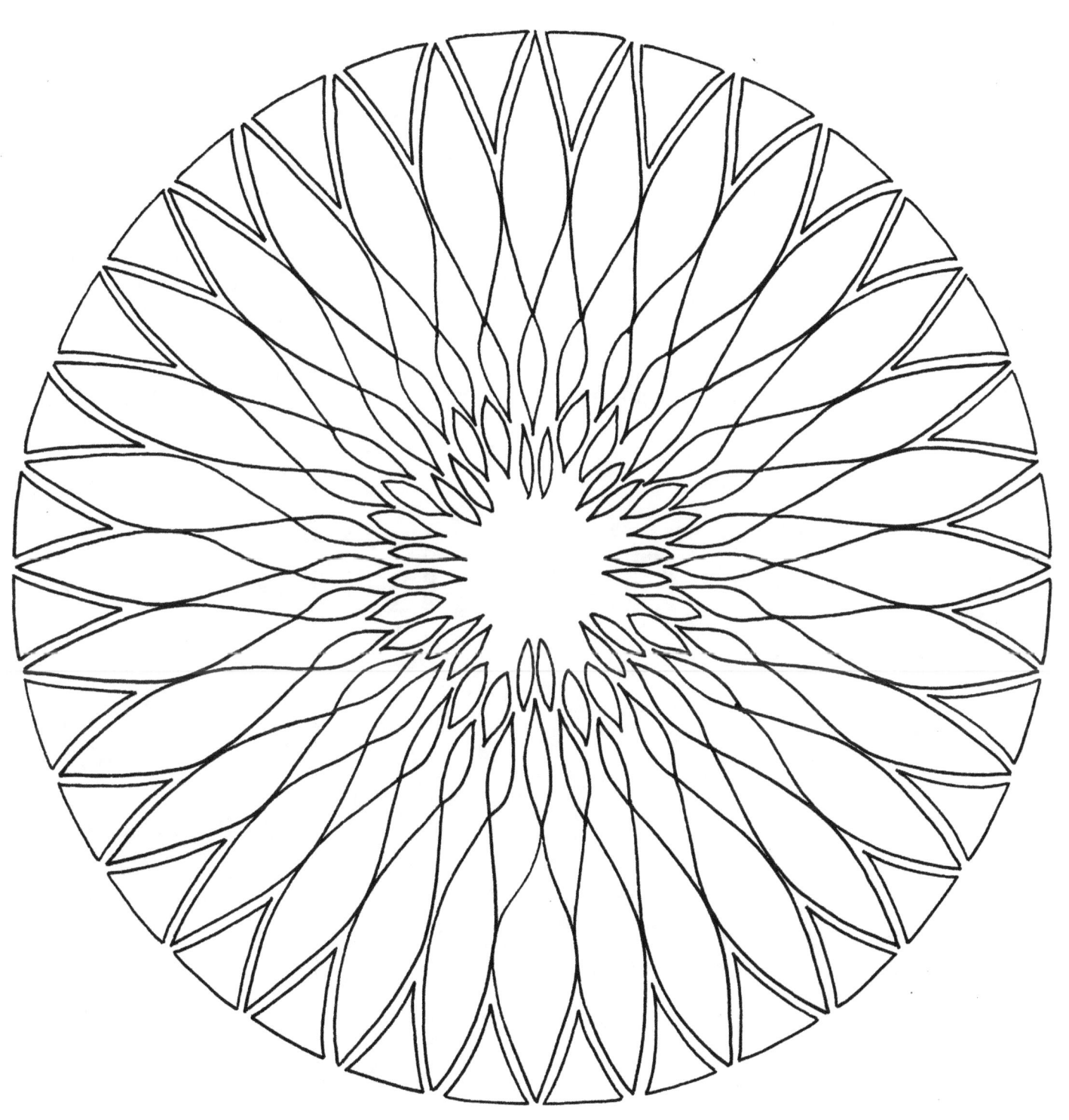

Title:

Date:

Artist:

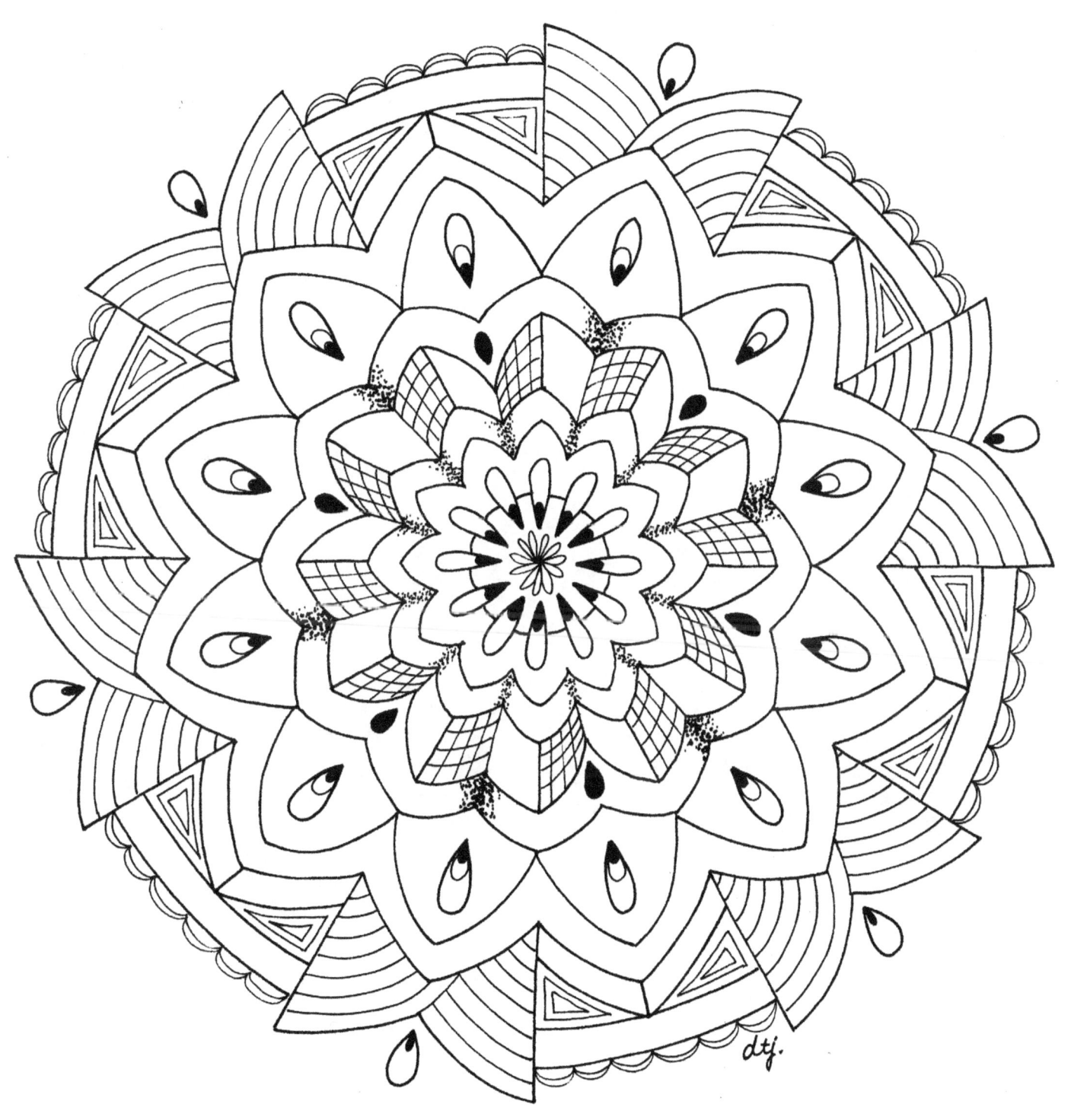

Title:

Date:

Colorist:

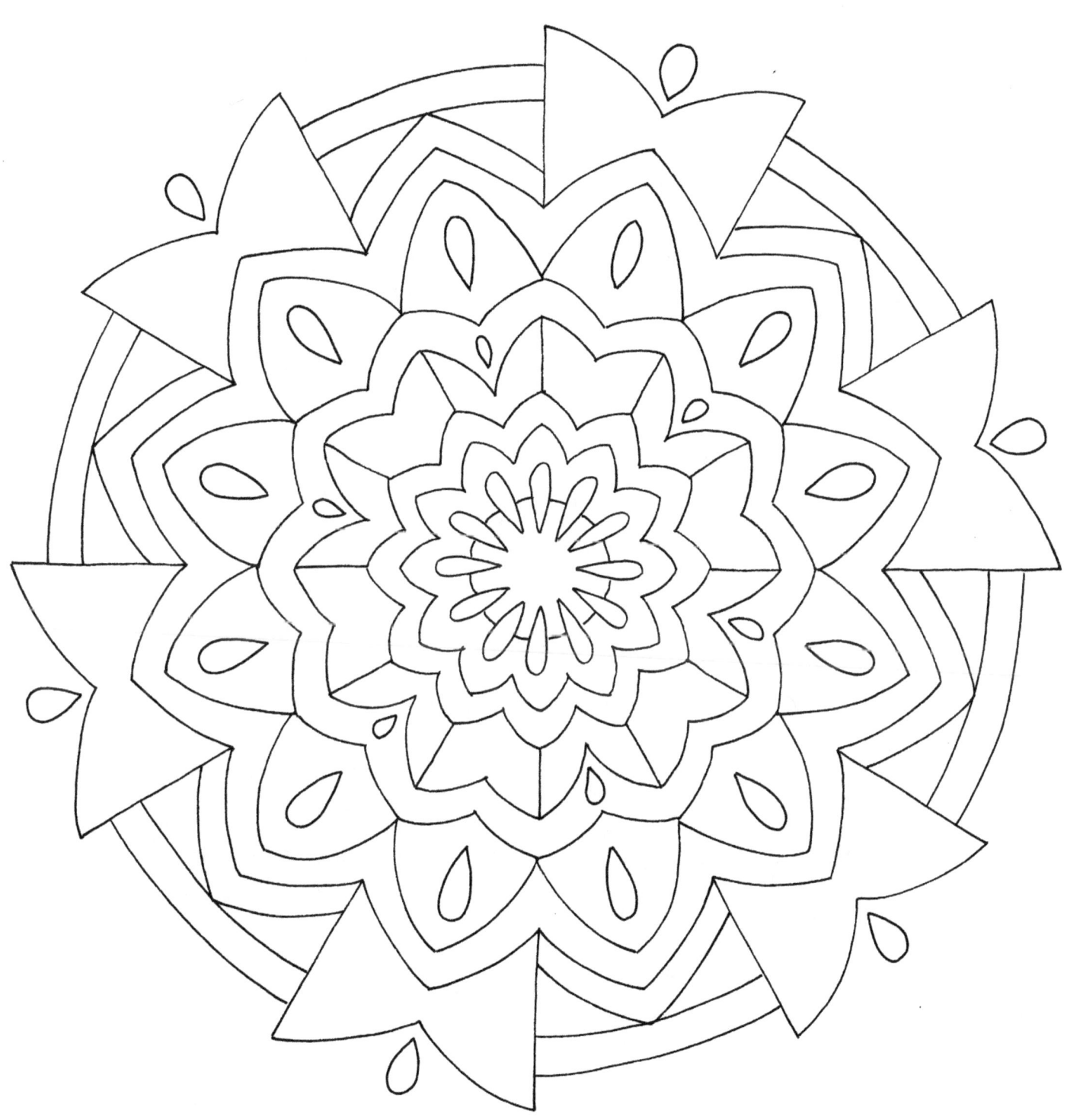

Title:

Date:

Artist:

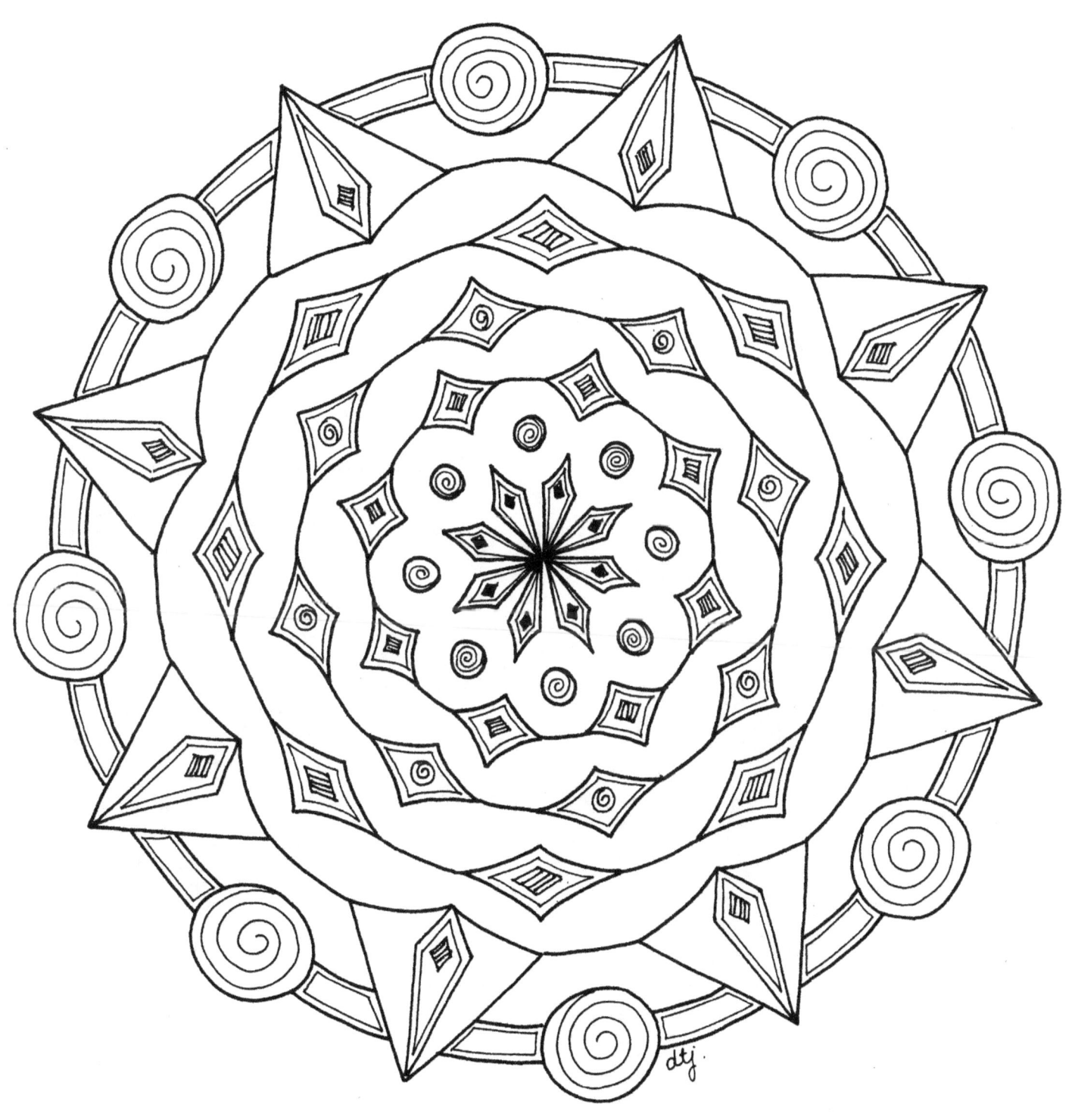

Title:

Date:

Colorist:

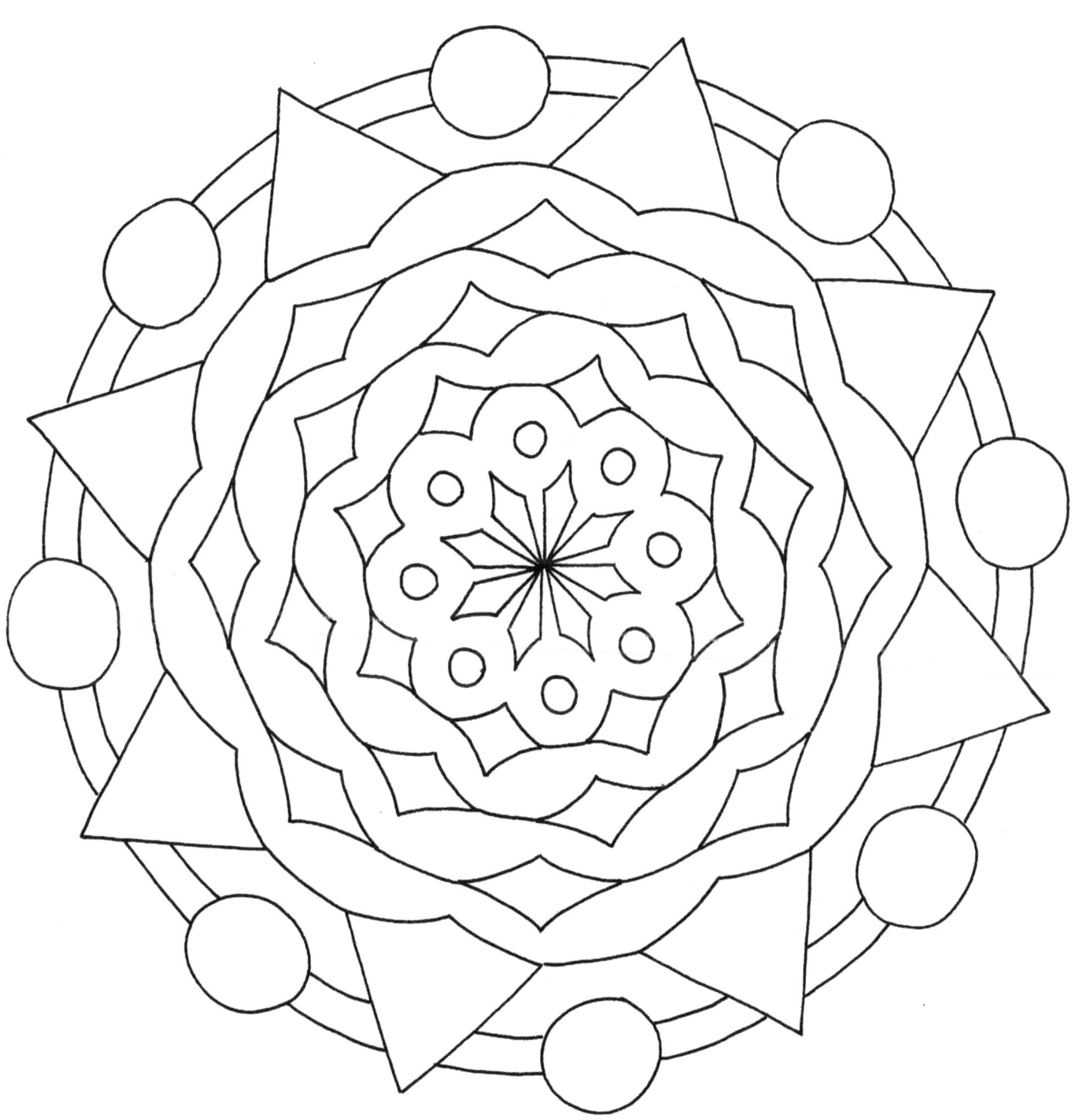

Title:

Date:

Artist:

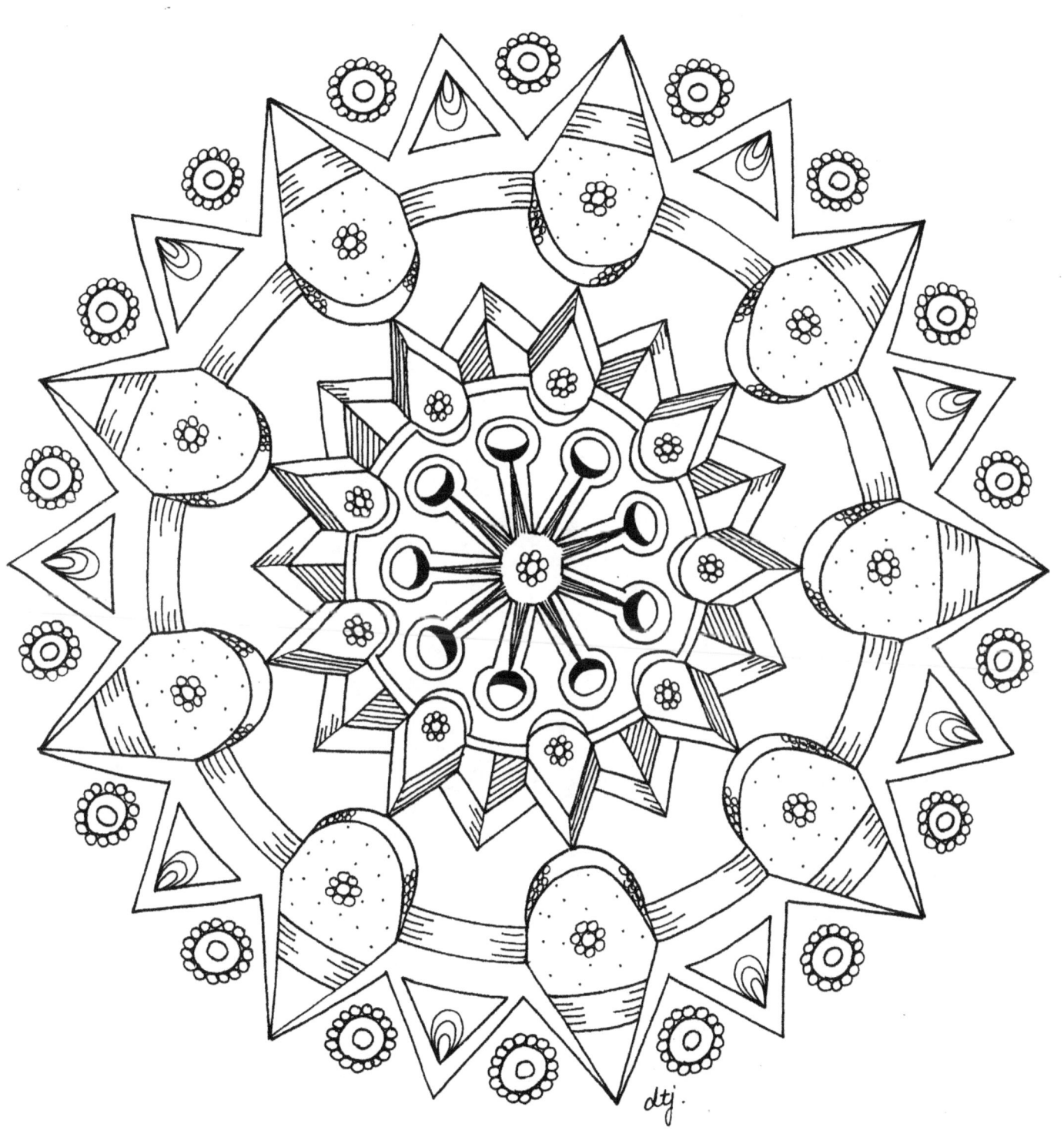

dtj.

Title:

Date:

Colorist:

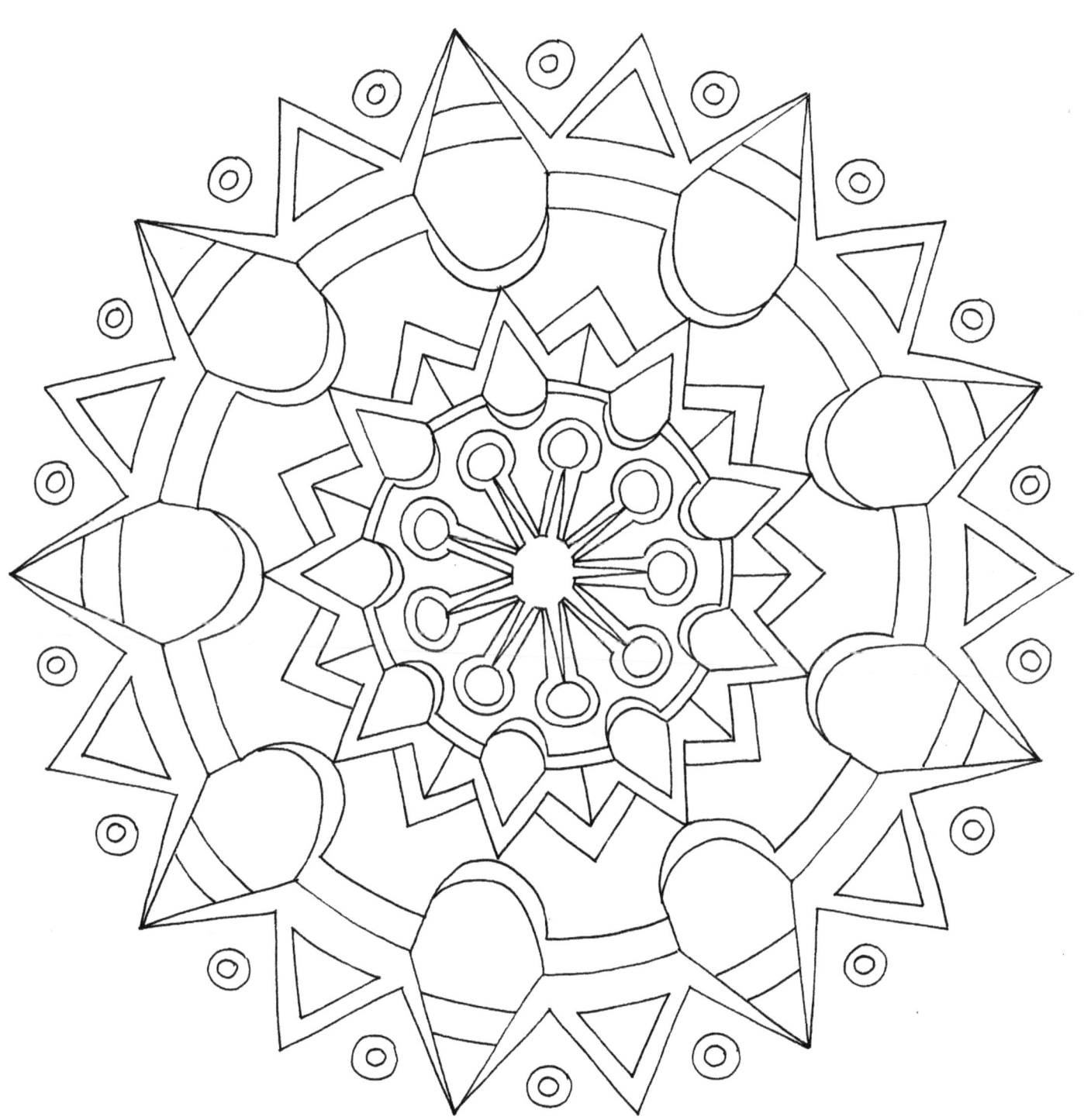

Title:

Date:

Artist:

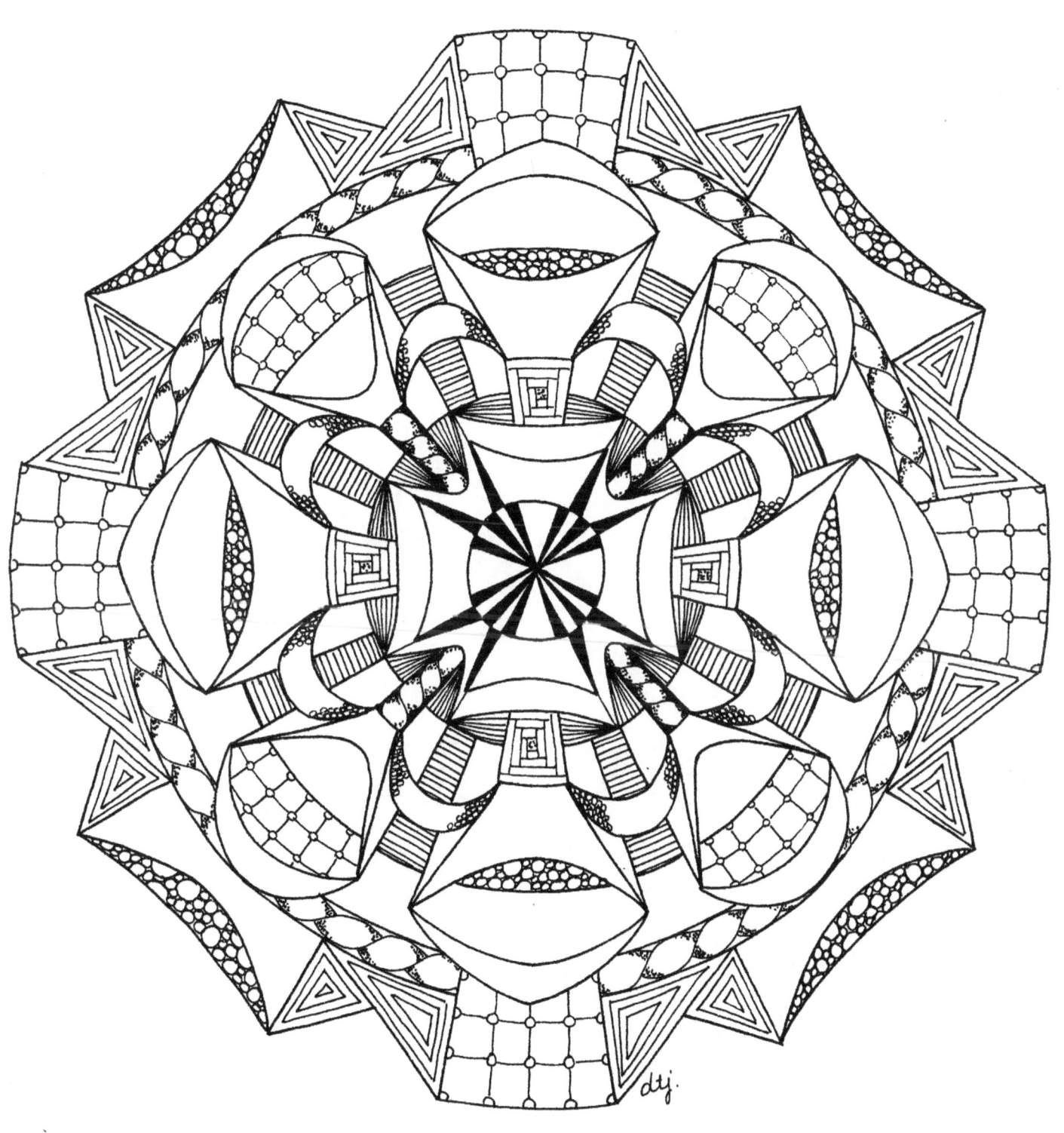

Title:

Date:

Colorist:

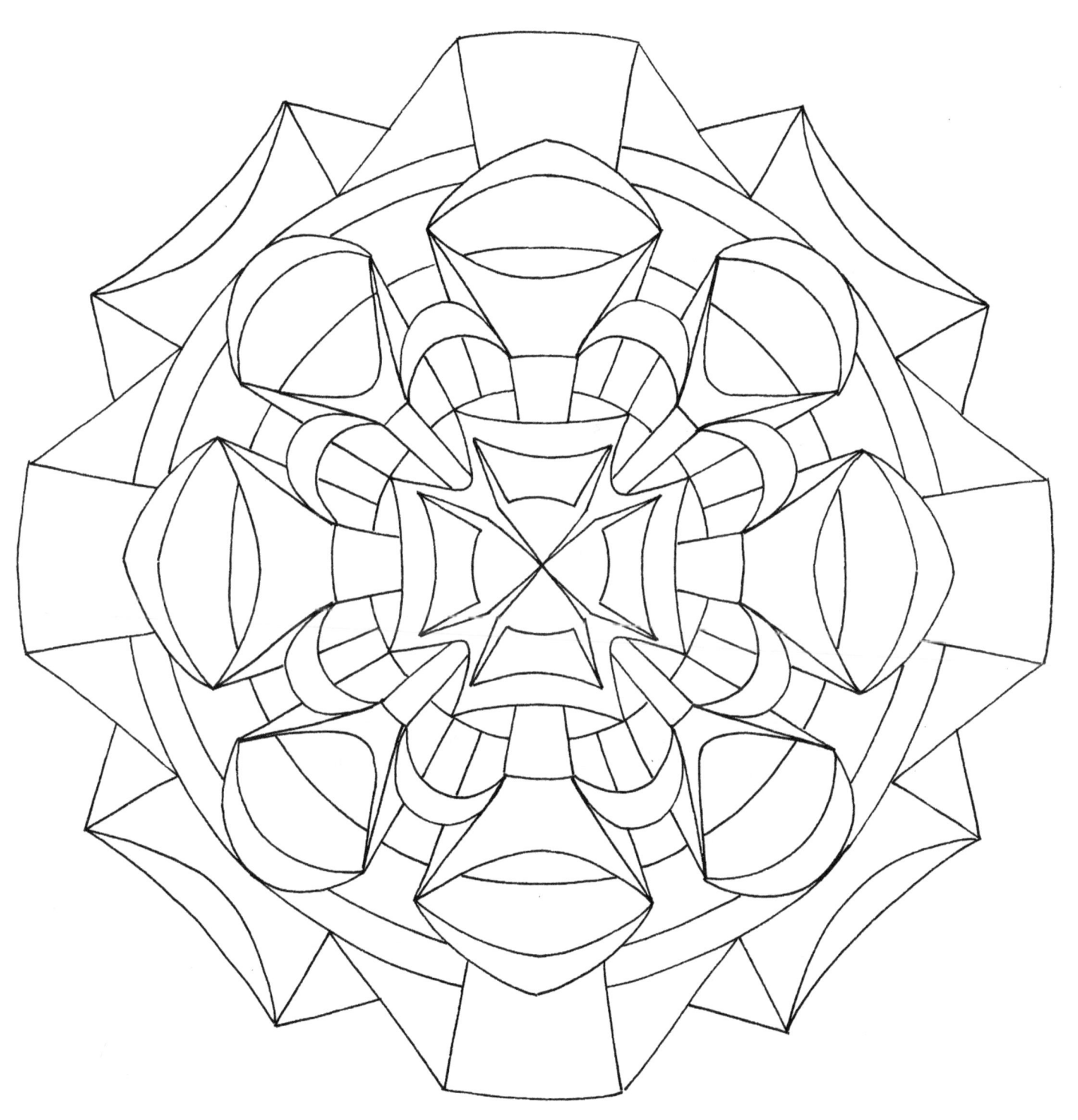

Title:

Date:

Artist:

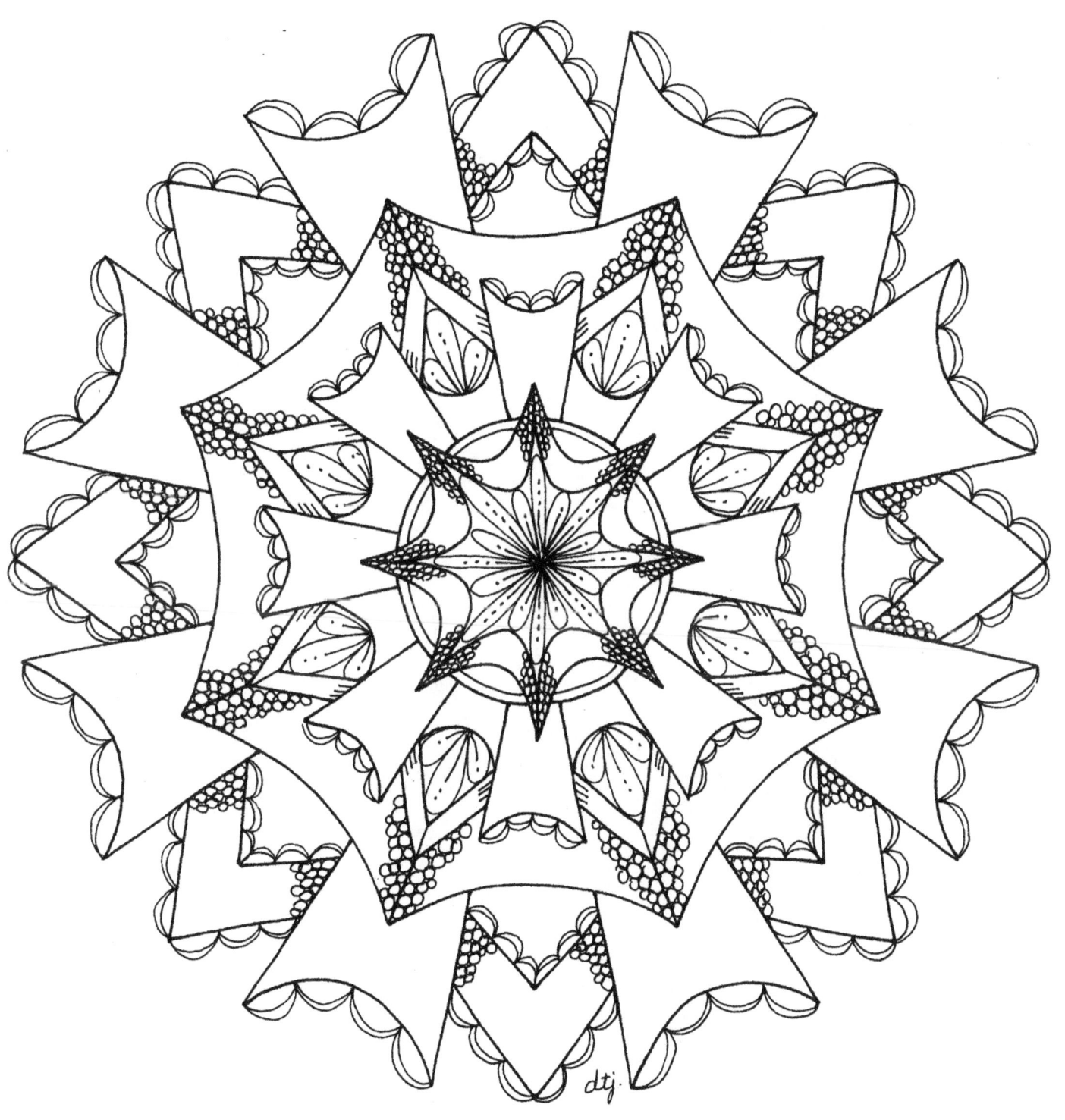

dtj.

Title:

Date:

Colorist:

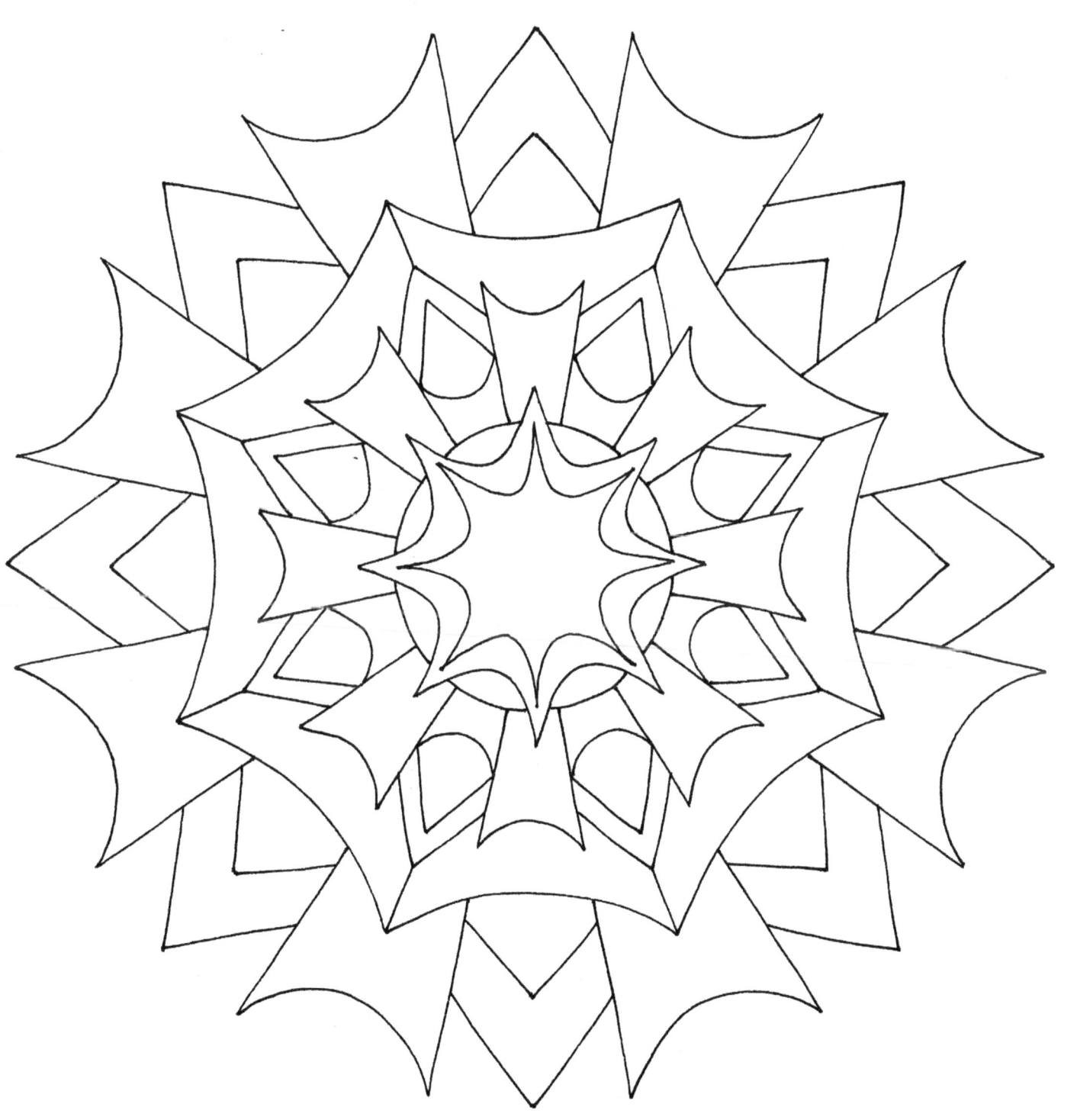

Title: _____

Date: _____

Artist: _____

_____

_____

_____

_____

_____

_____

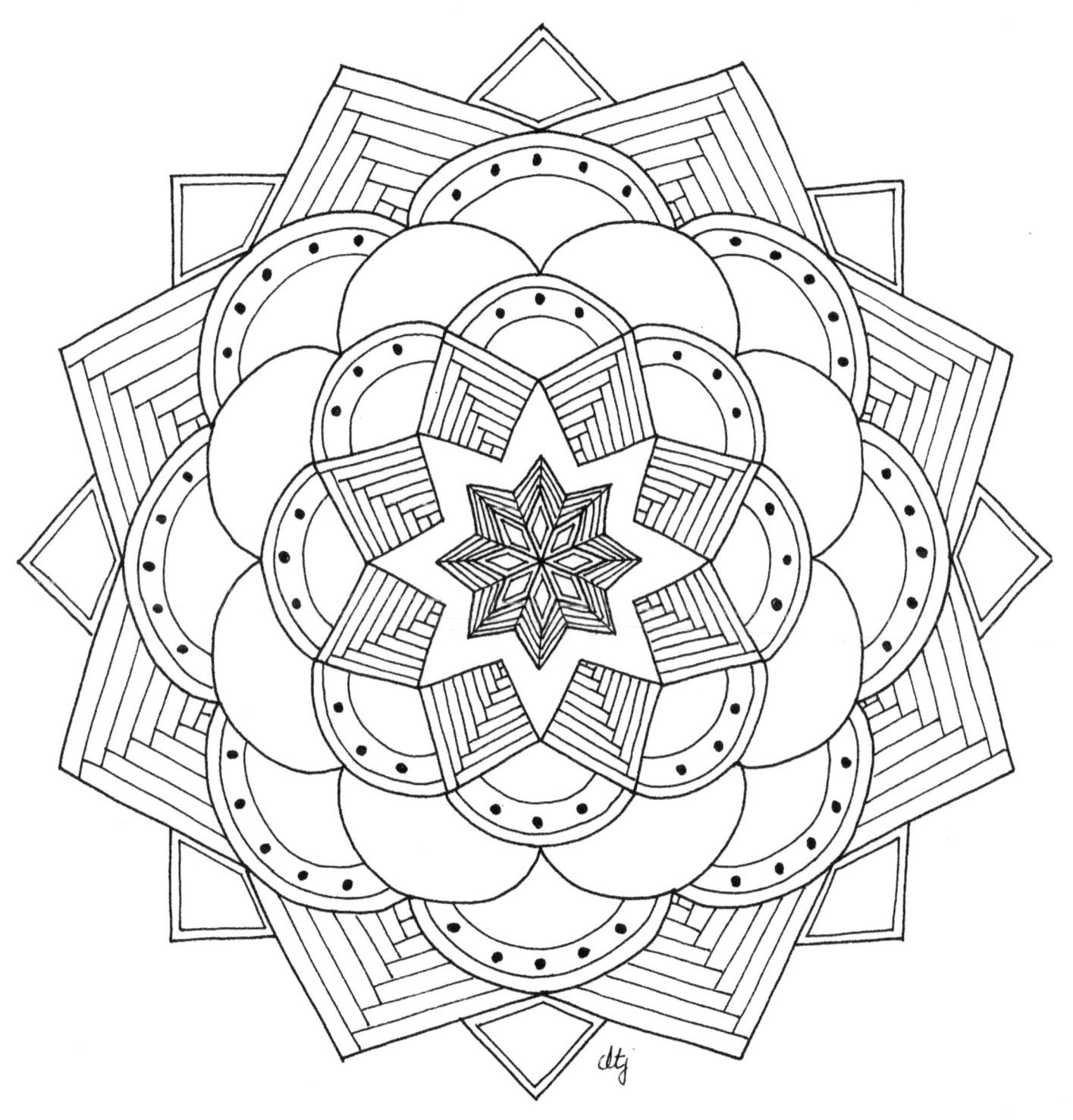

Title:

Date:

Colorist:

32

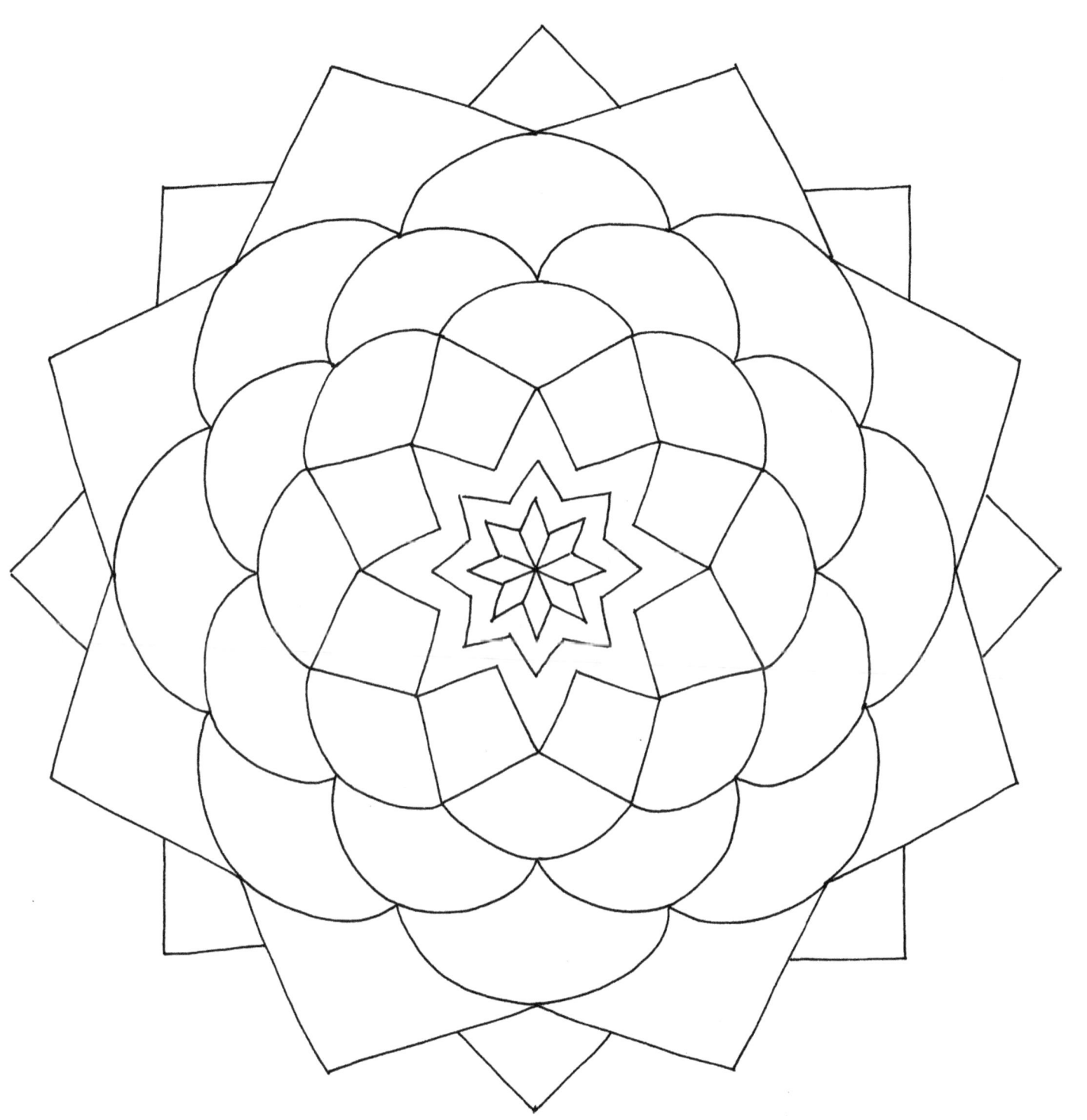

Title:

Date:

Artist:

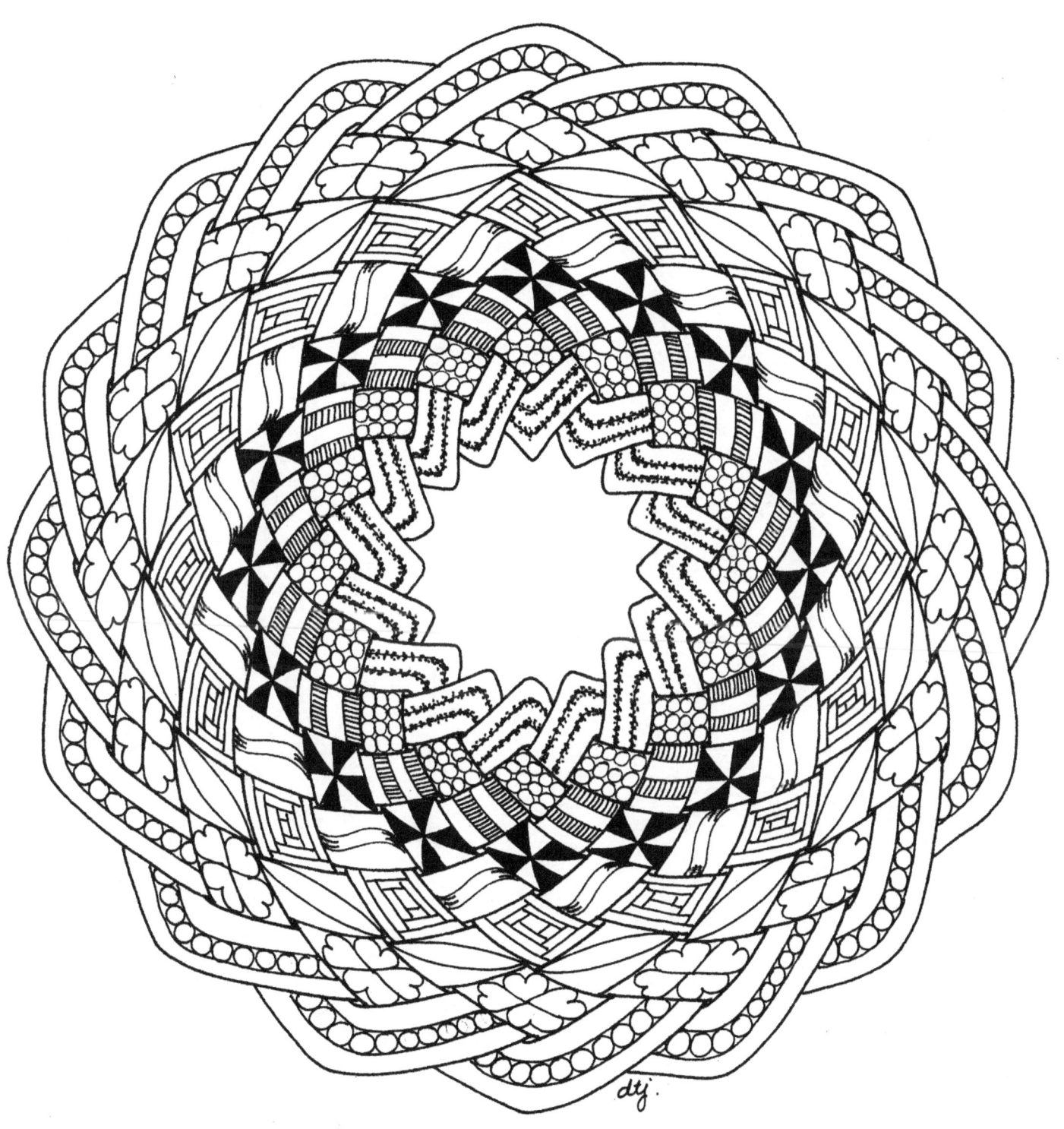

Title:

Date:

Colorist:

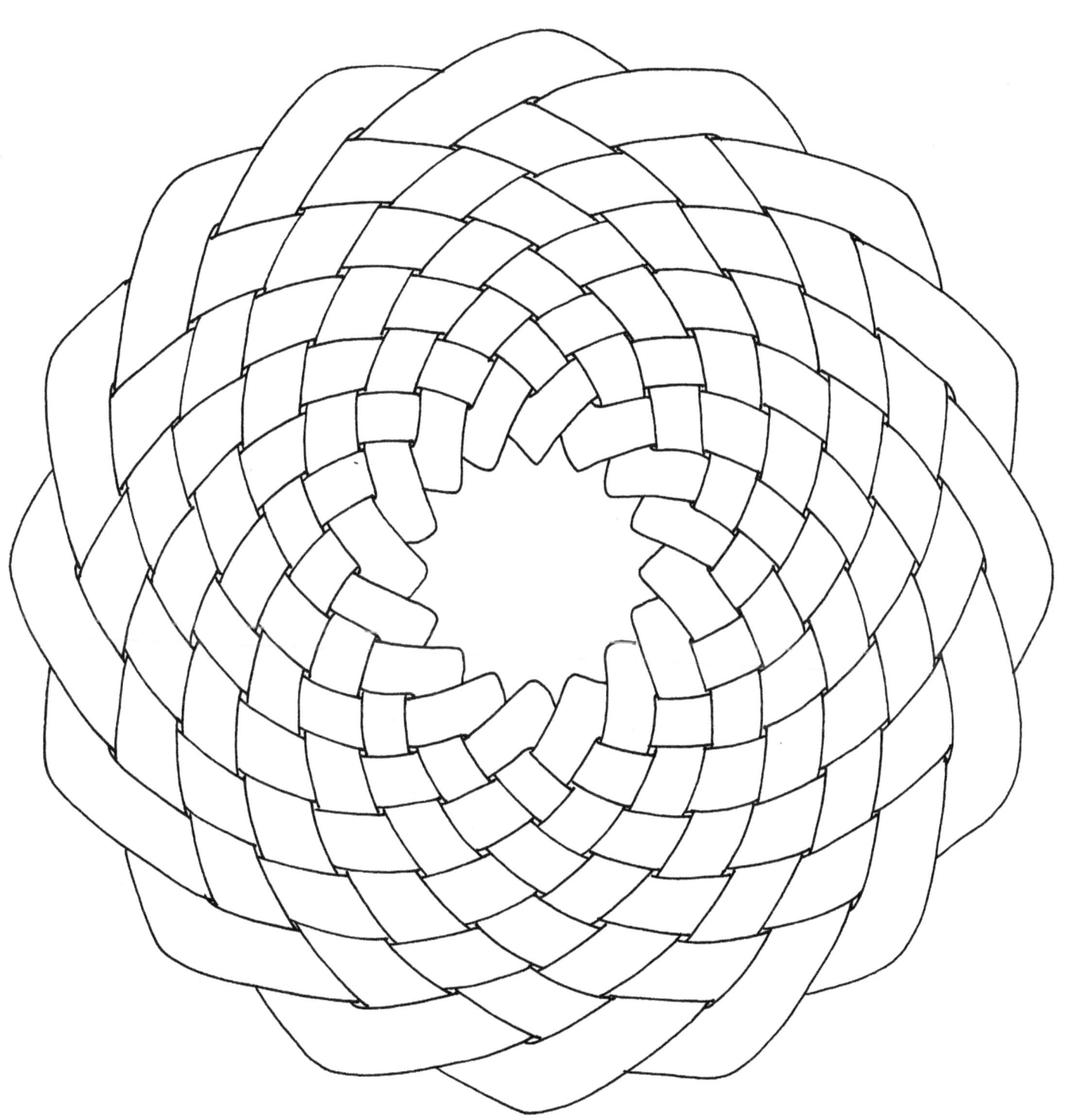

Title:

Date:

Colorist:

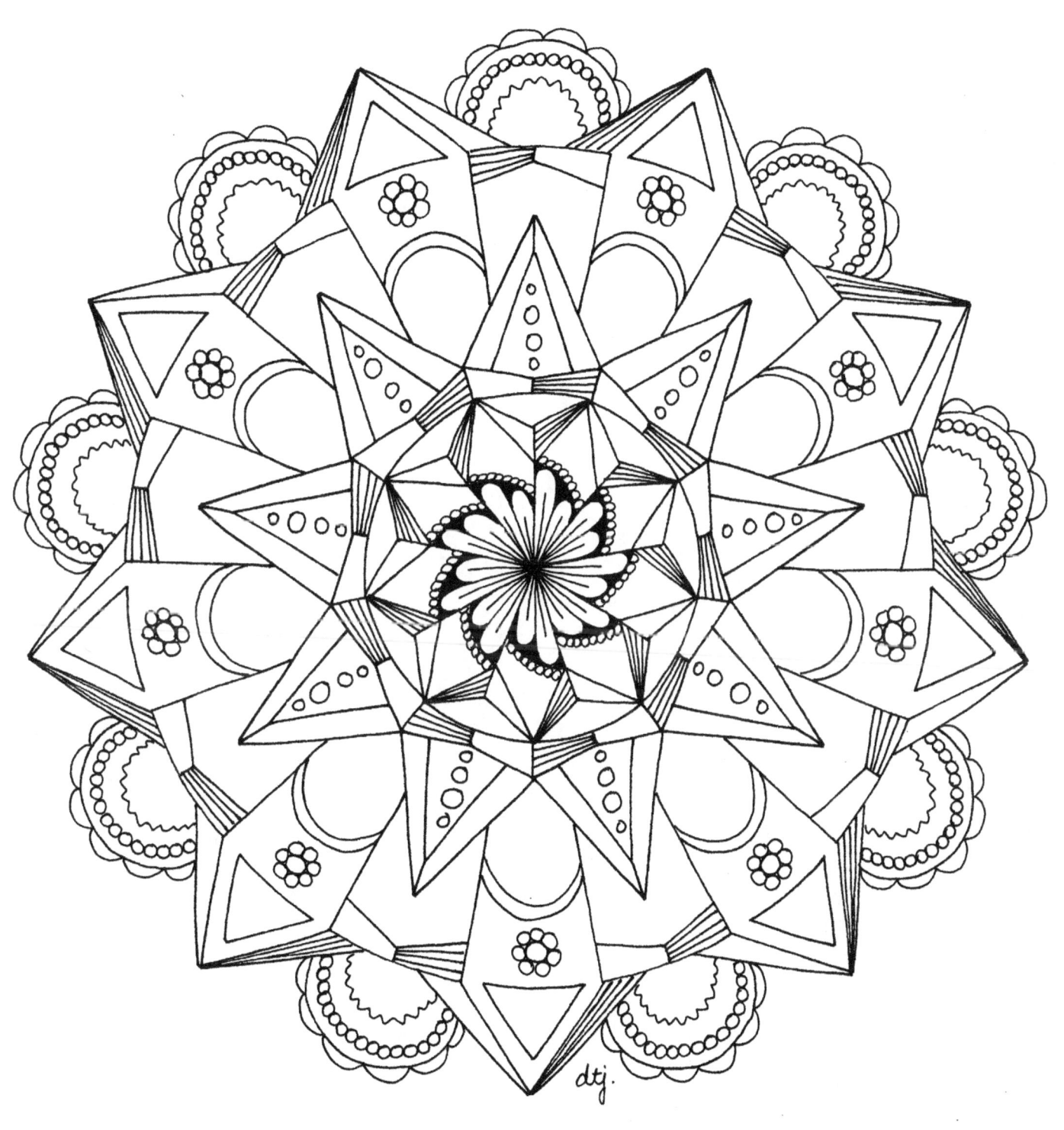

Title:

Date:

Colorist:

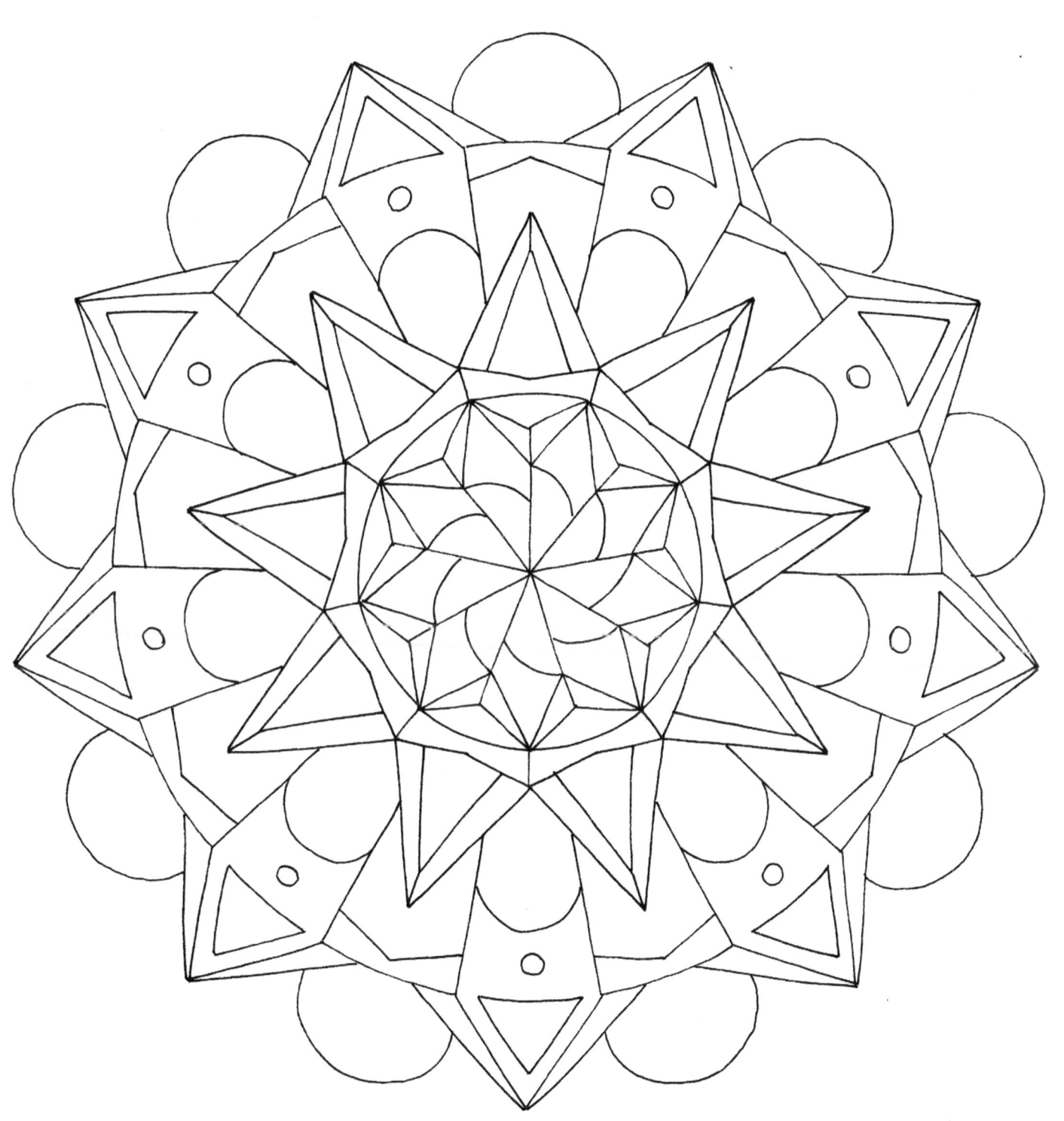

Title:

Date:

Artist:

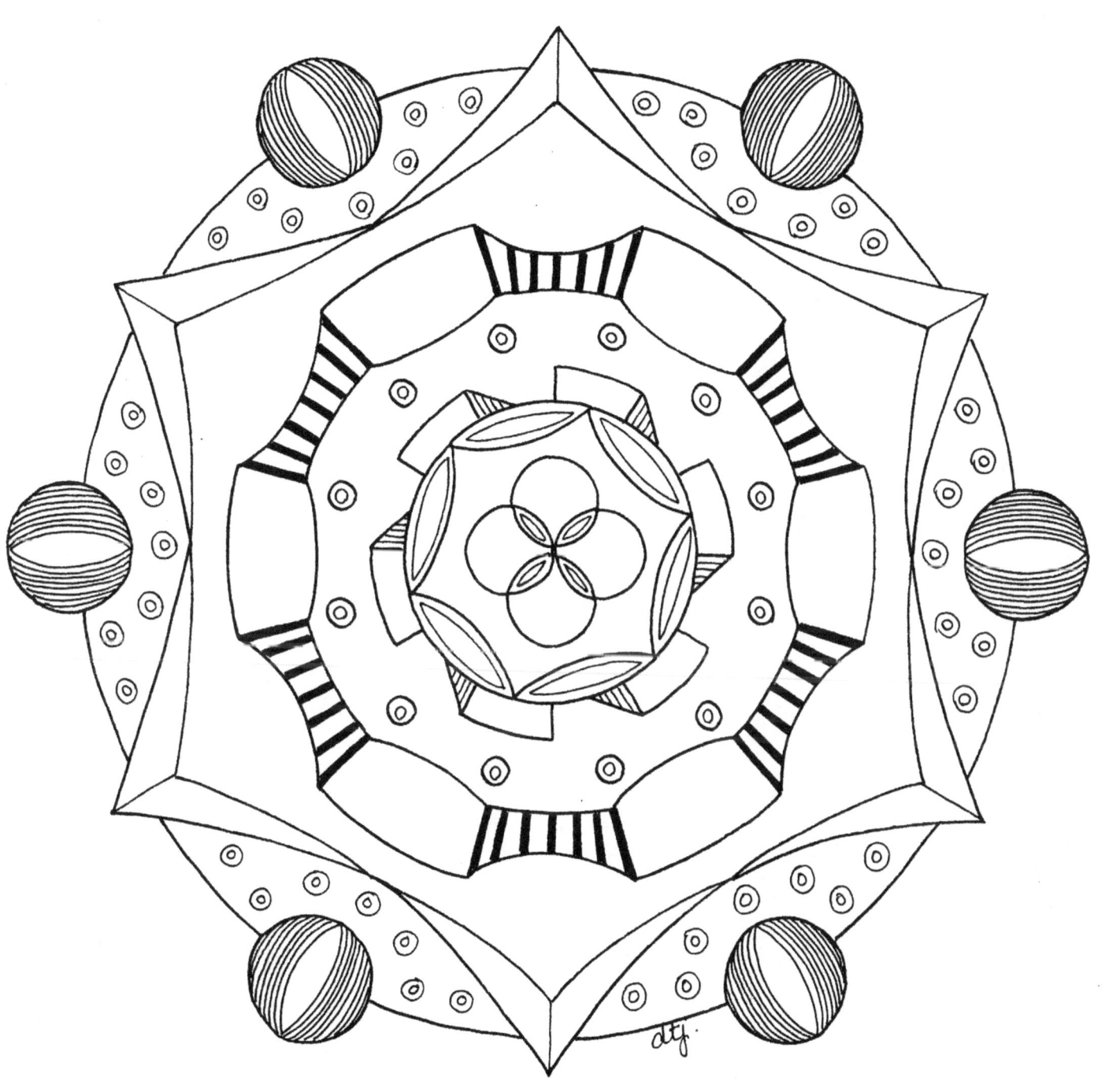

Title:

Date:

Colorist:

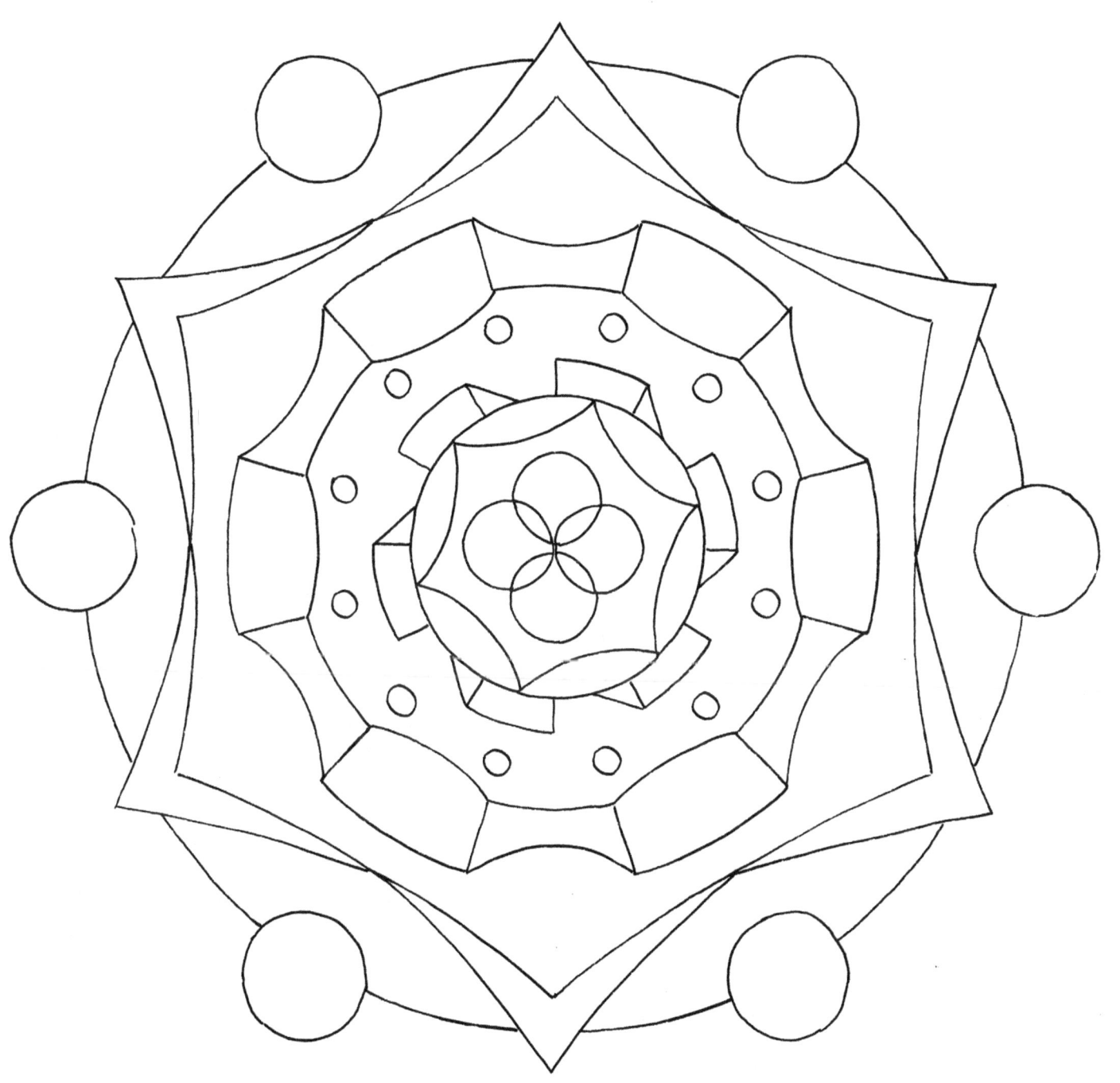

Title:

Date:

Artist:

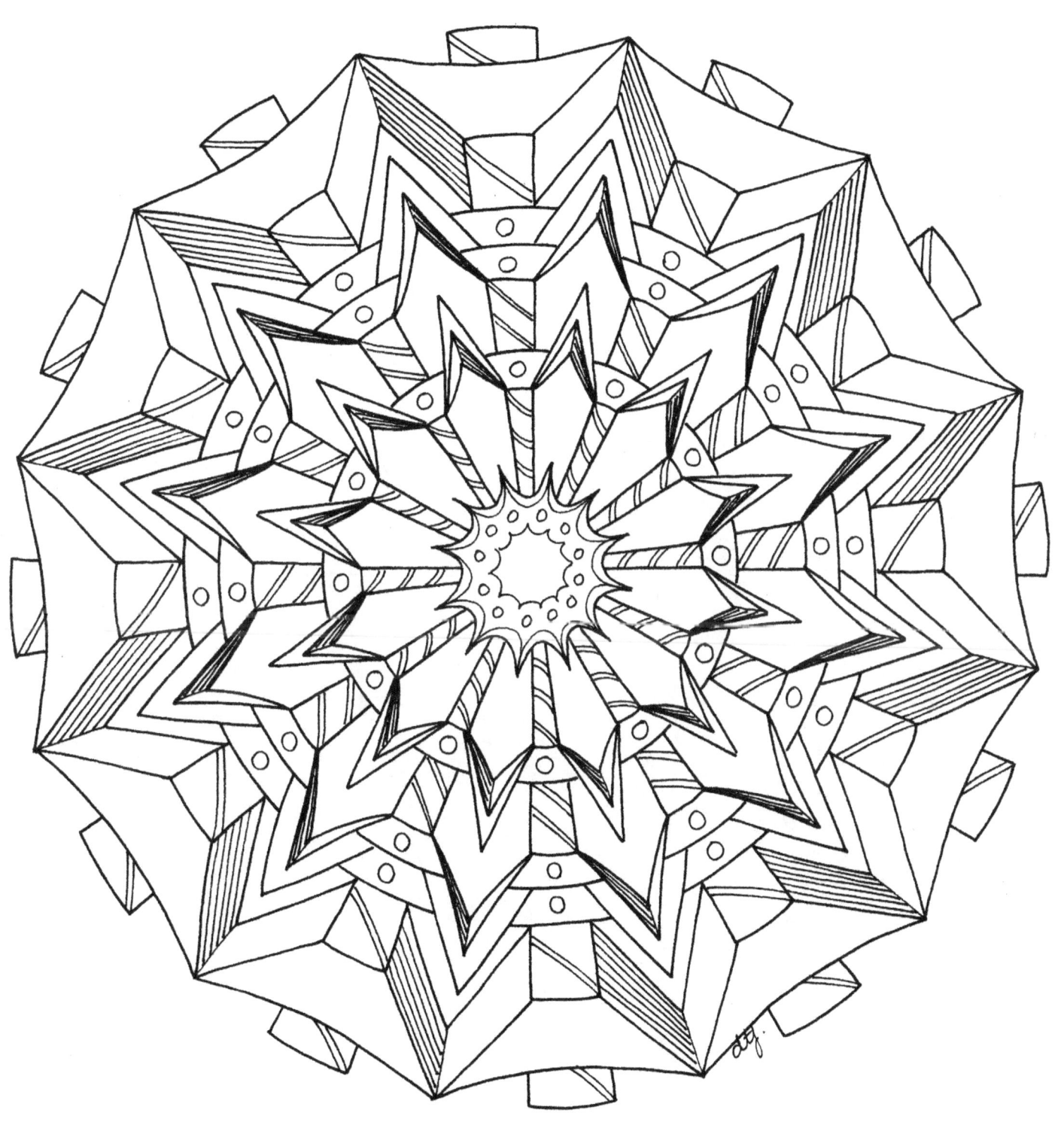

Title:

Date:

Colorist:

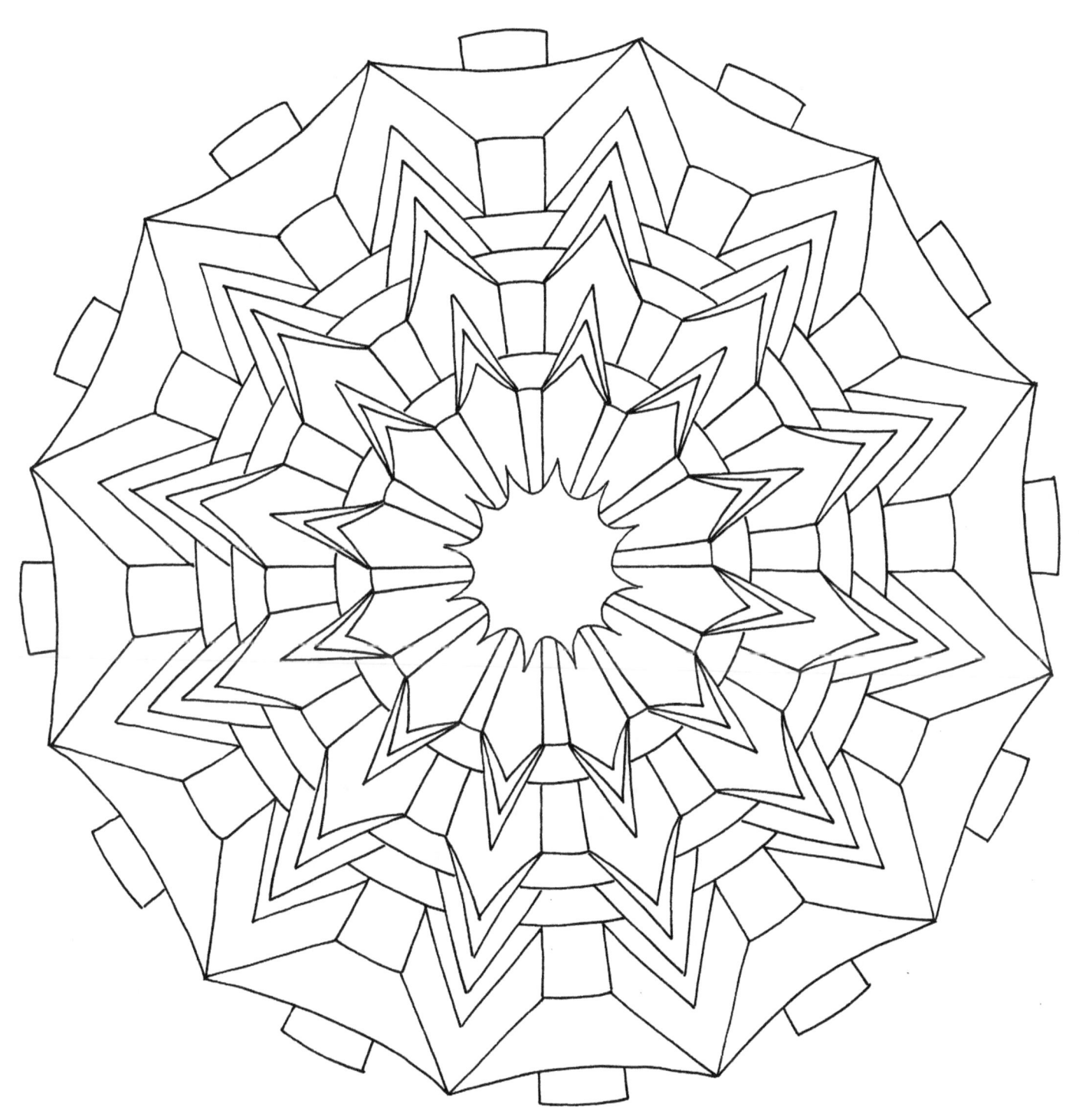

Title:

Date:

Artist:

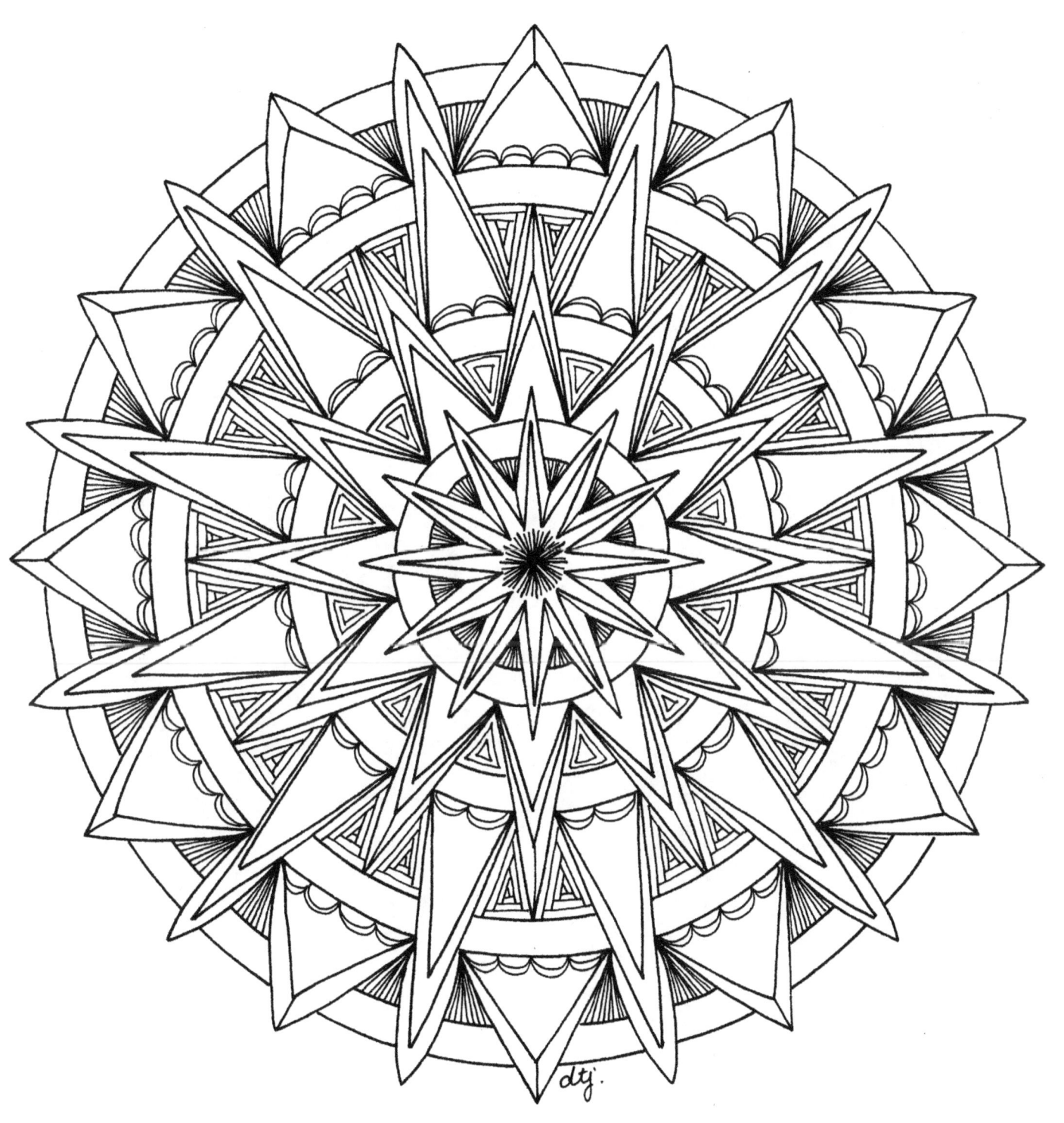

Title:

Date:

Artist:

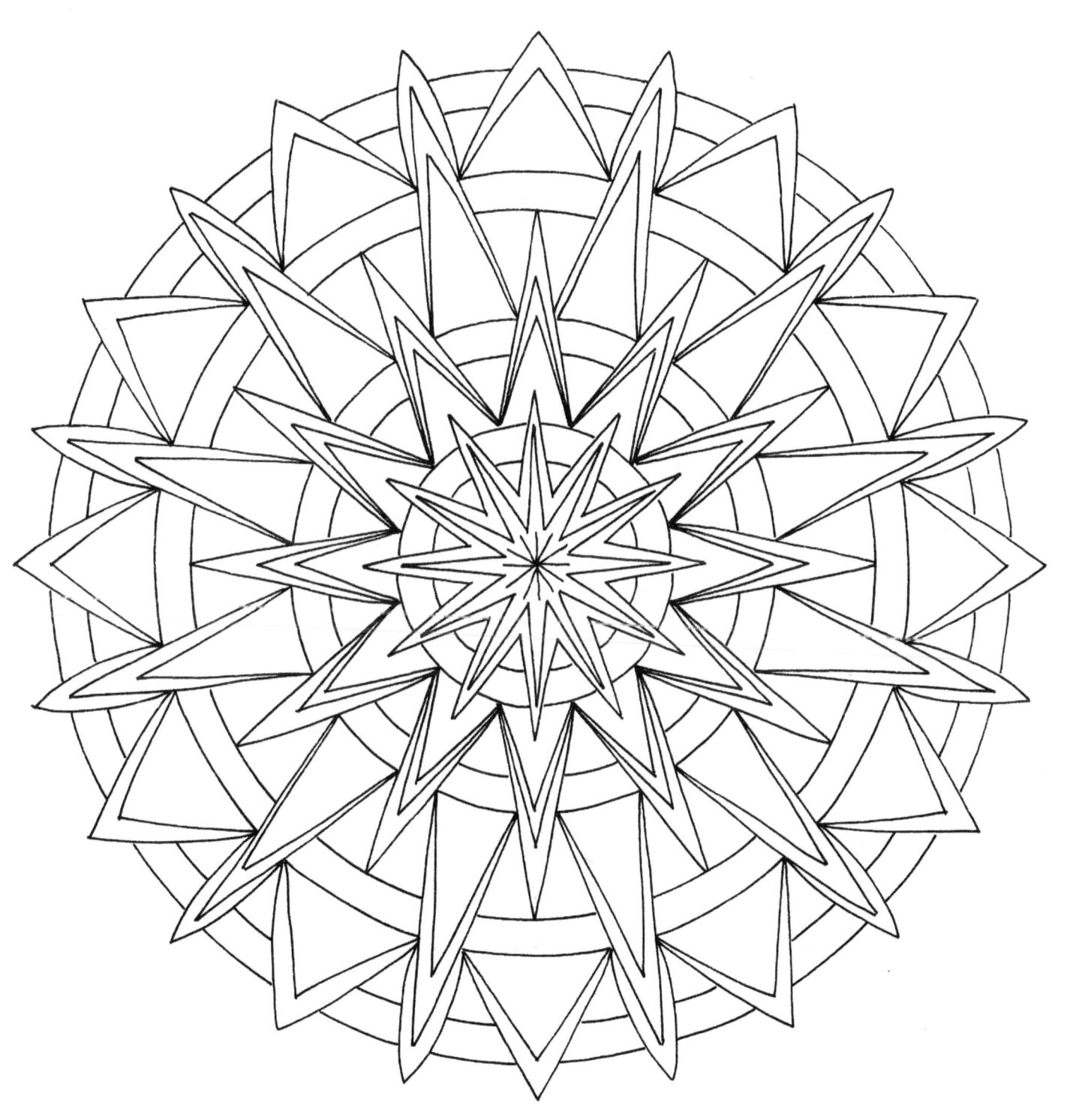

Title:

Date:

Colorist:

54

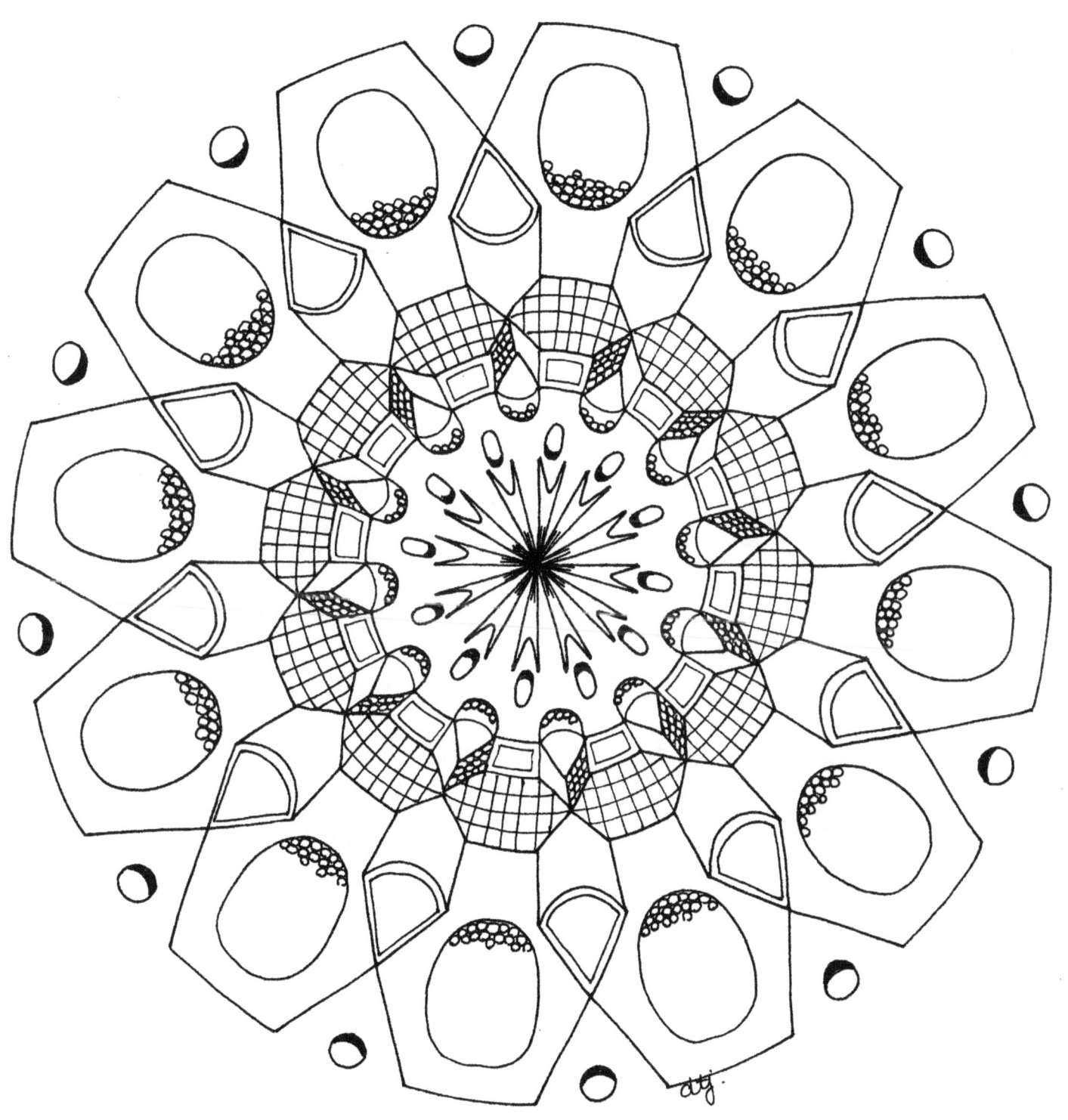

55

Title:

Date:

Colorist:

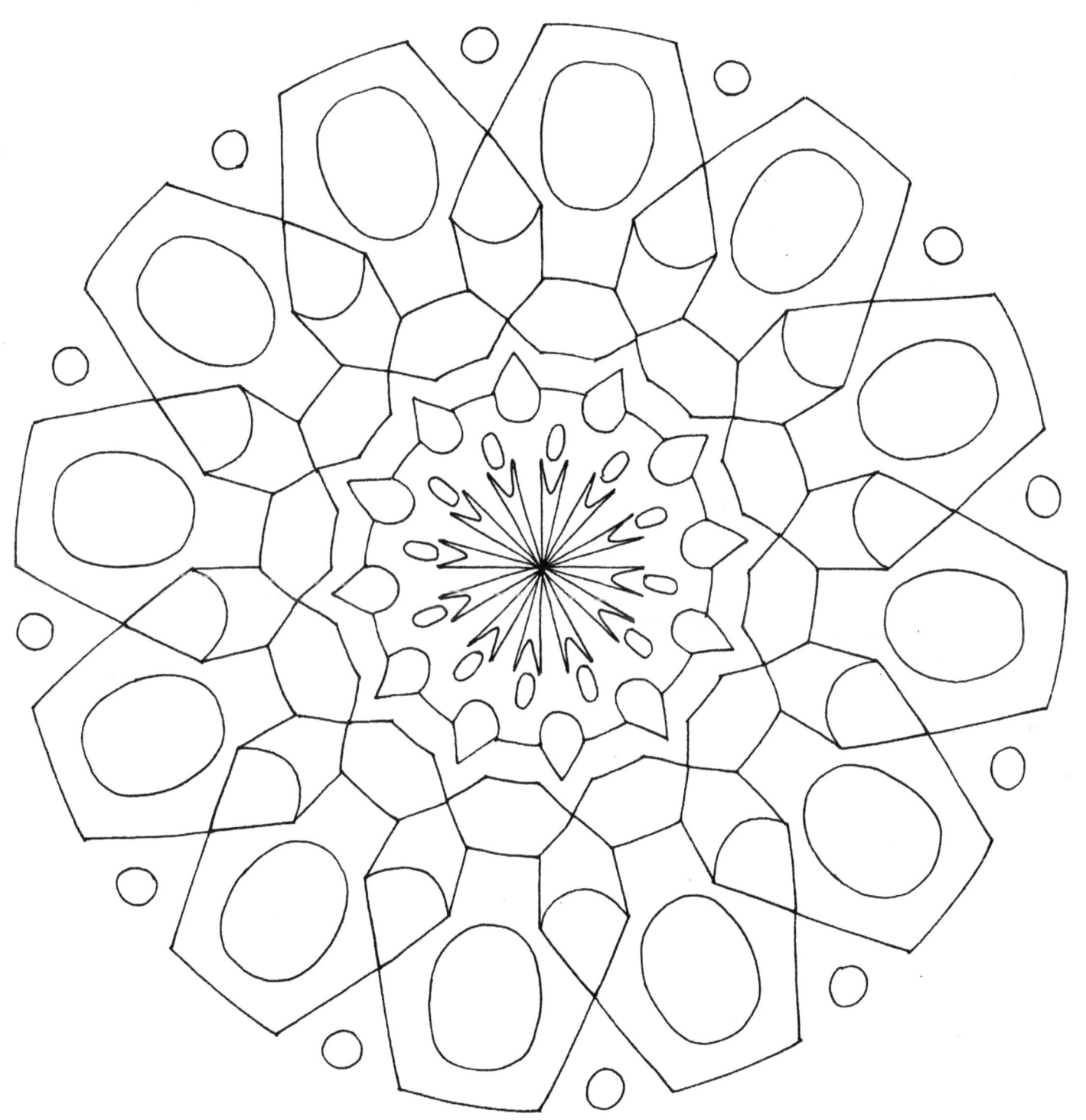

Title:

Date:

Artist:

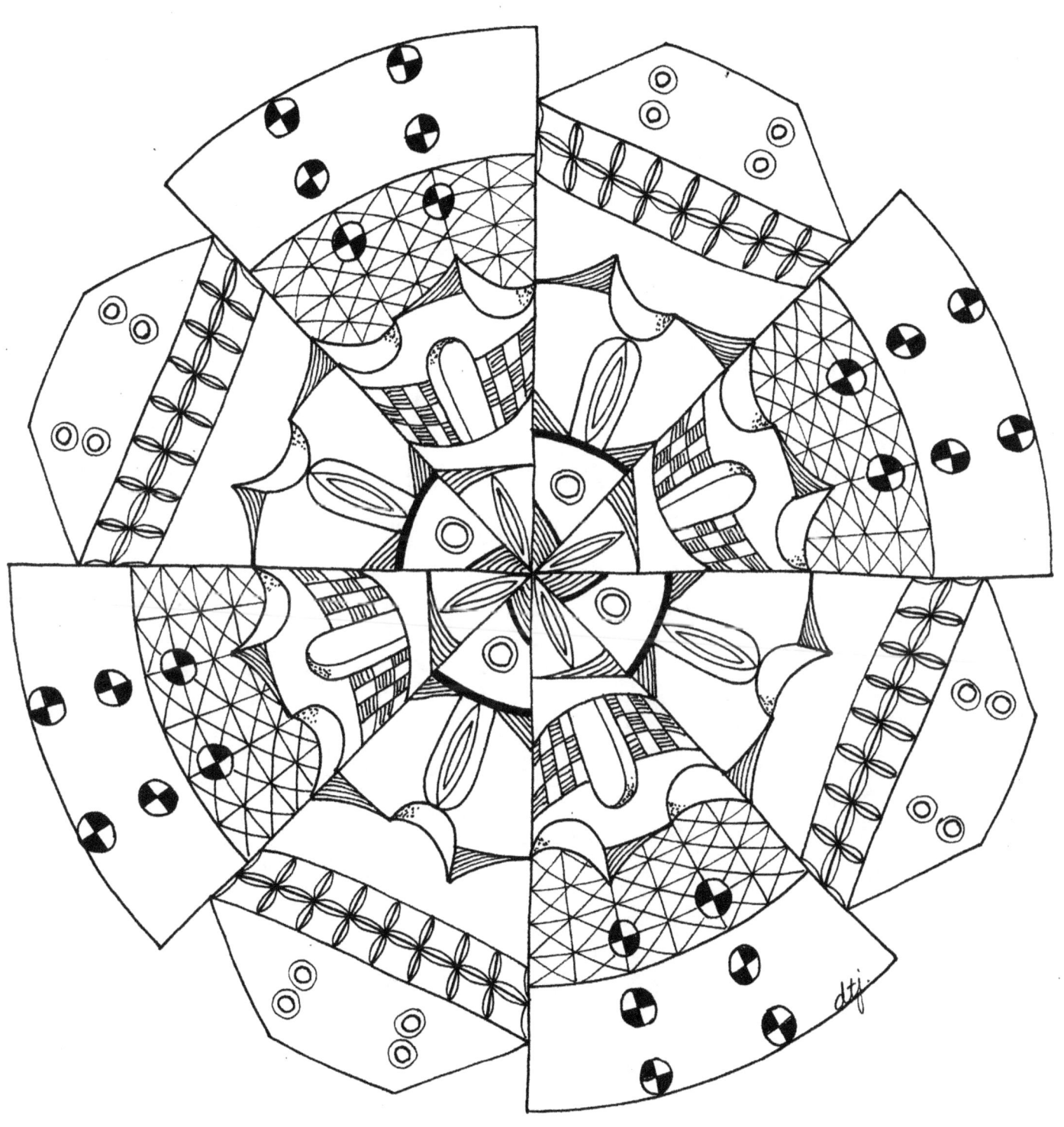

Title:

Date:

Colorist:

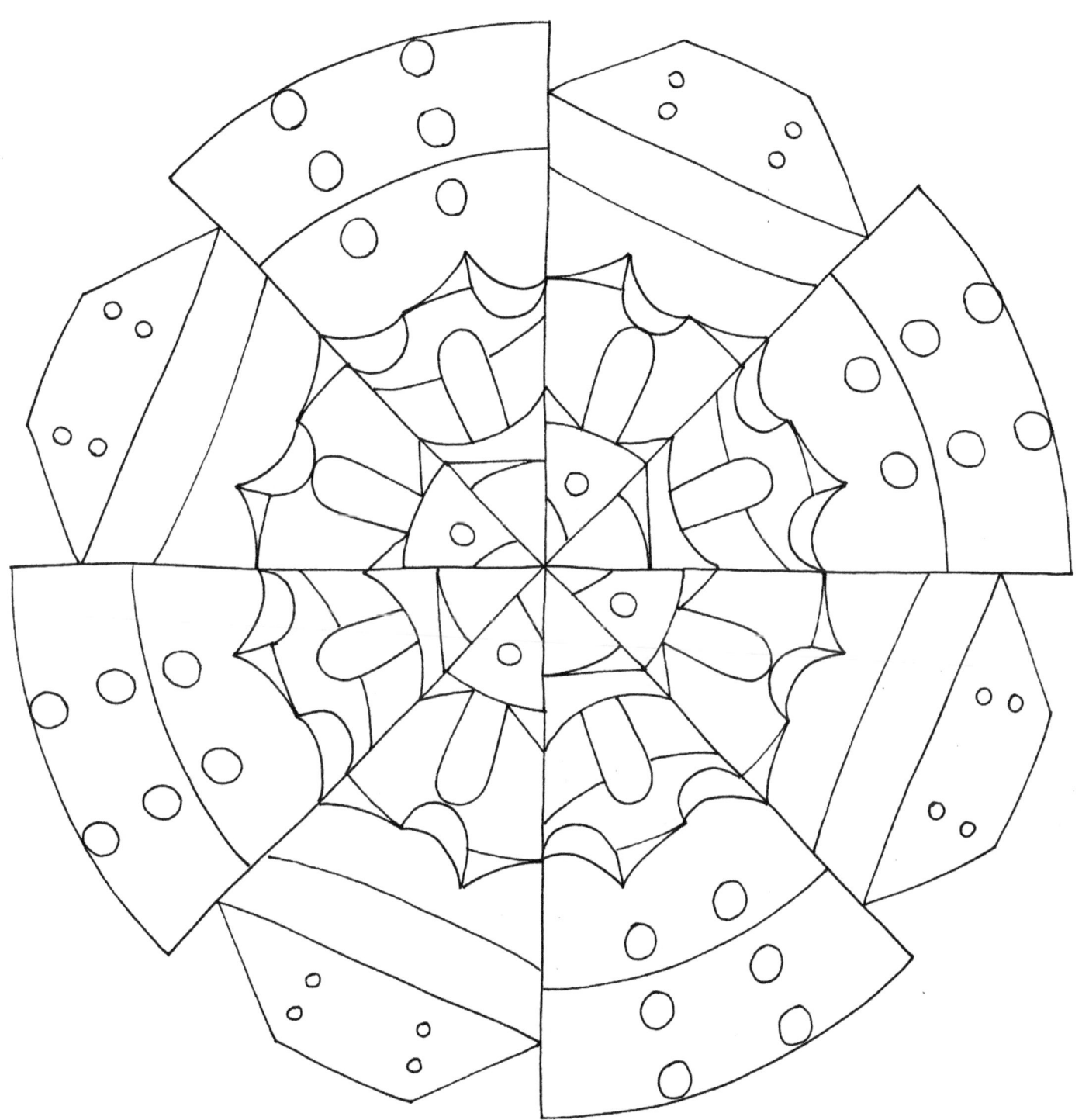

Title:

Date:

Artist:

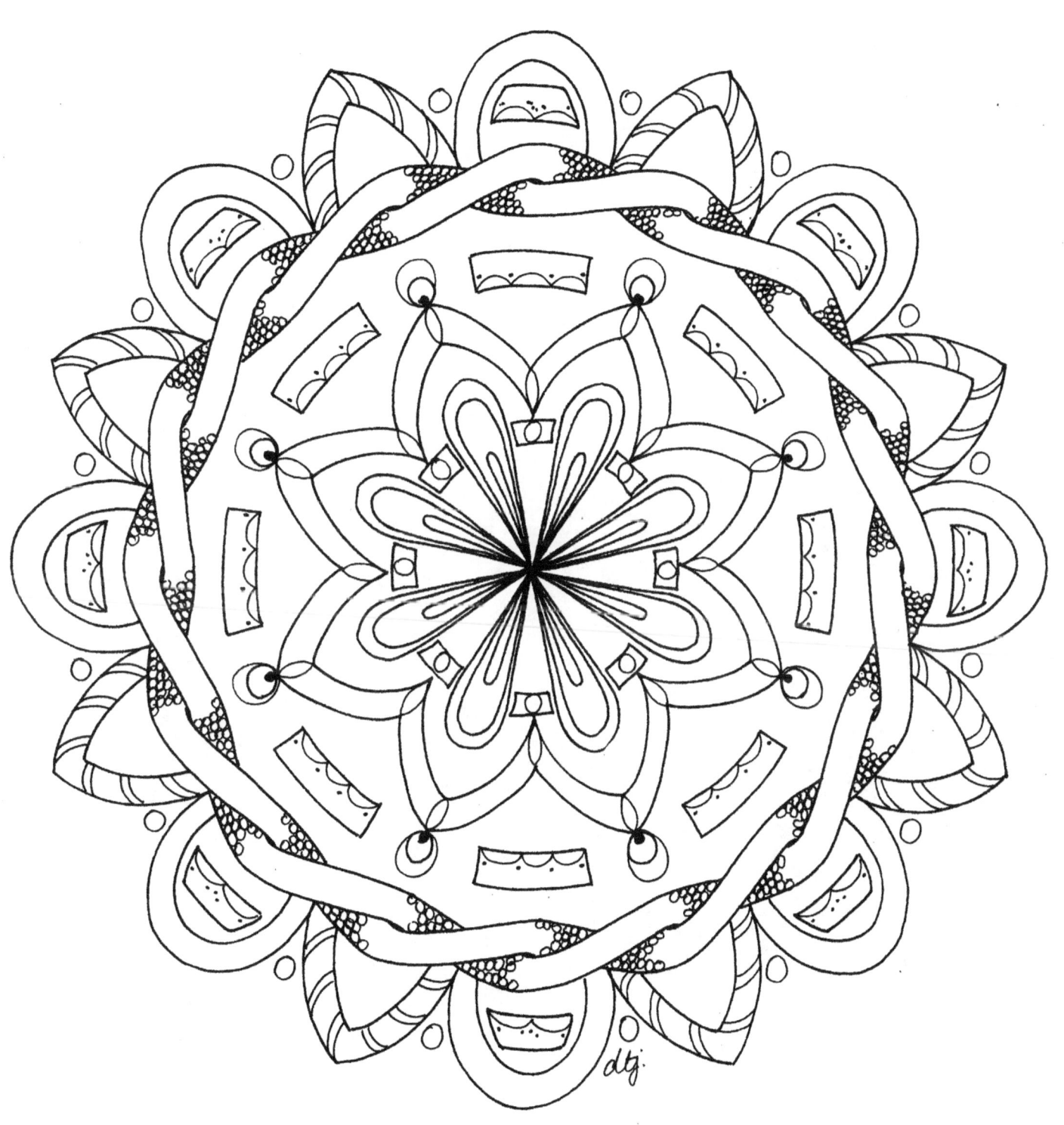

Title:

Date:

Colorist:

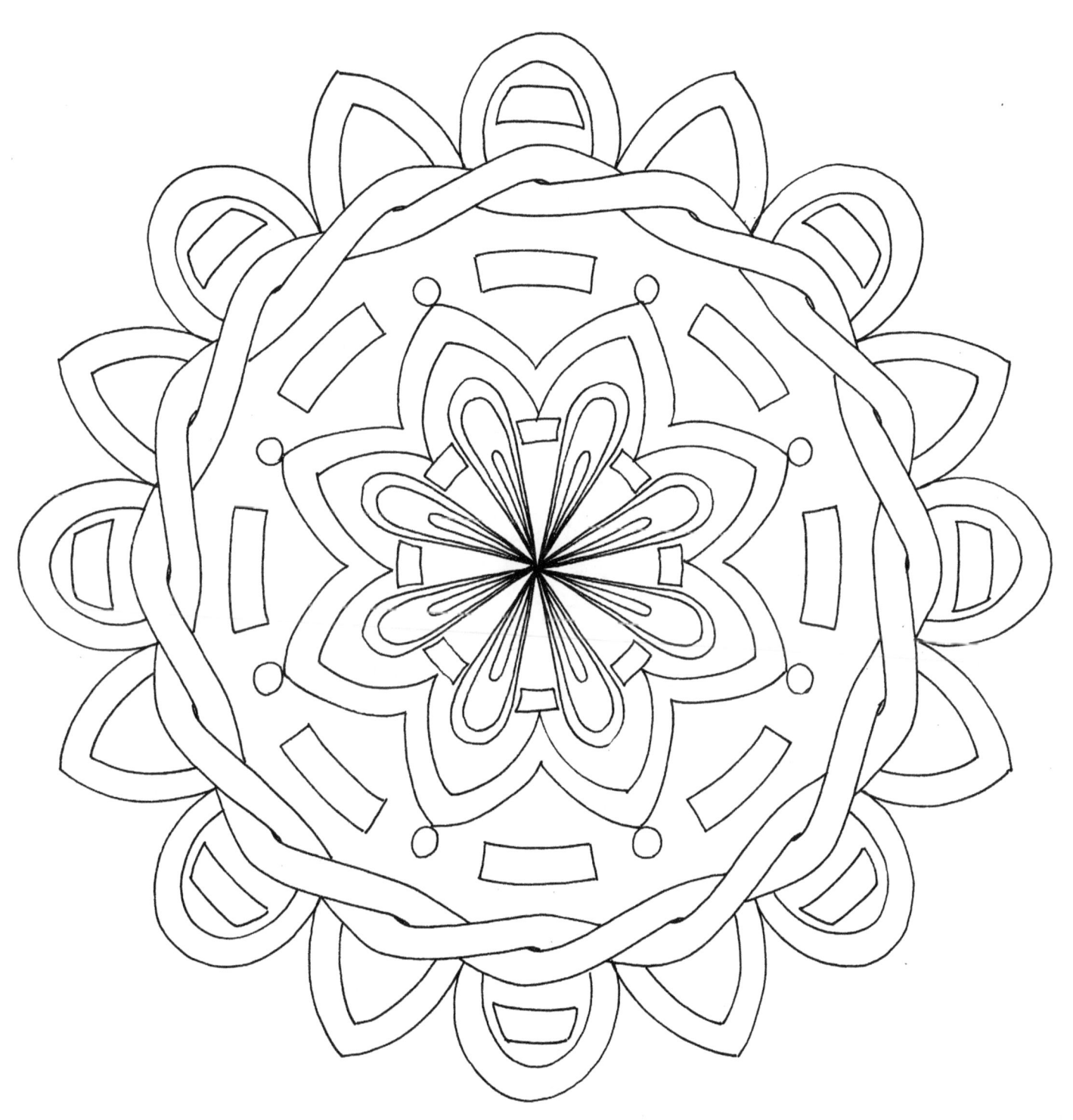

Title:

Date:

Artist:

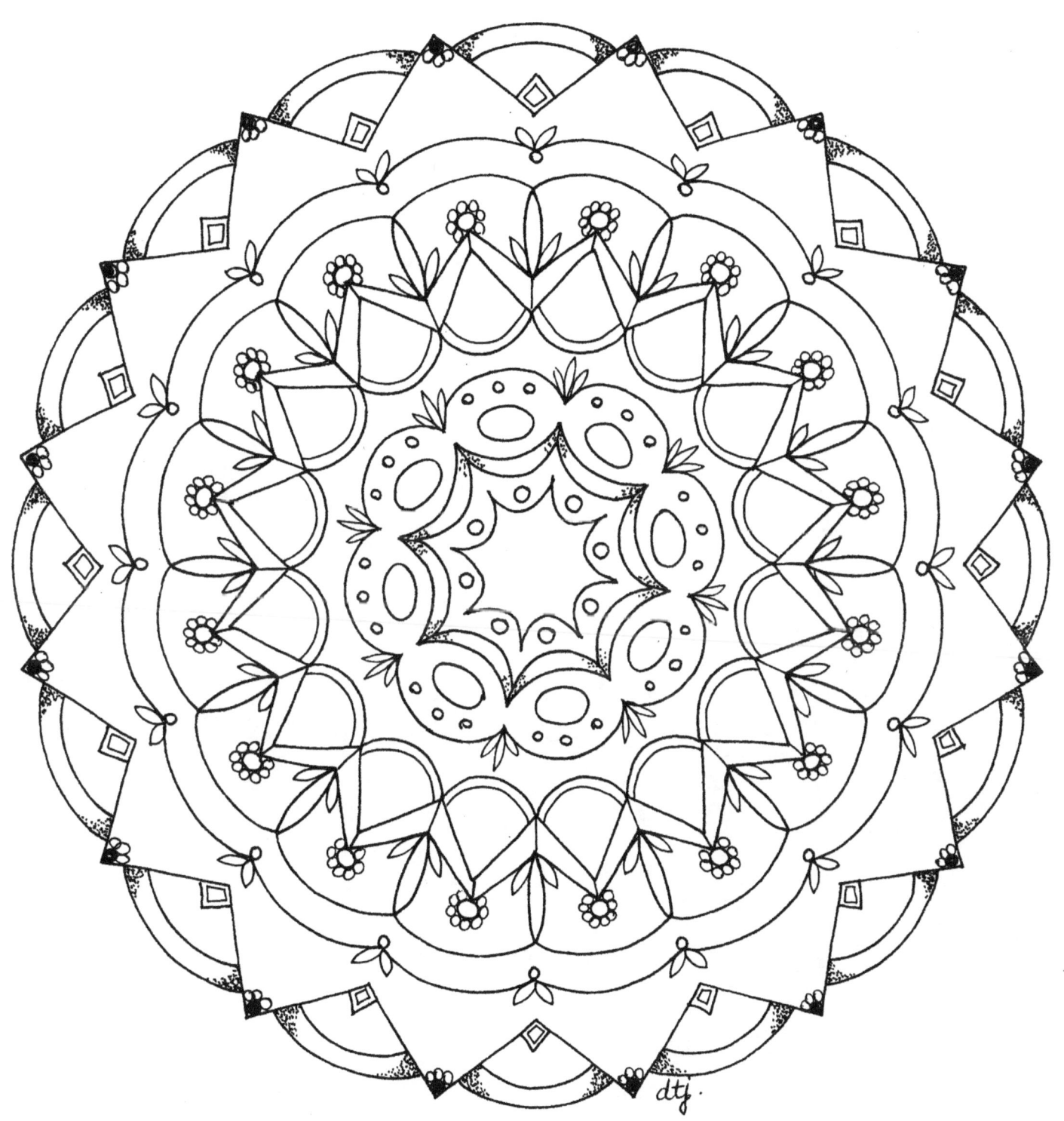

Title:

Date:

Colorist:

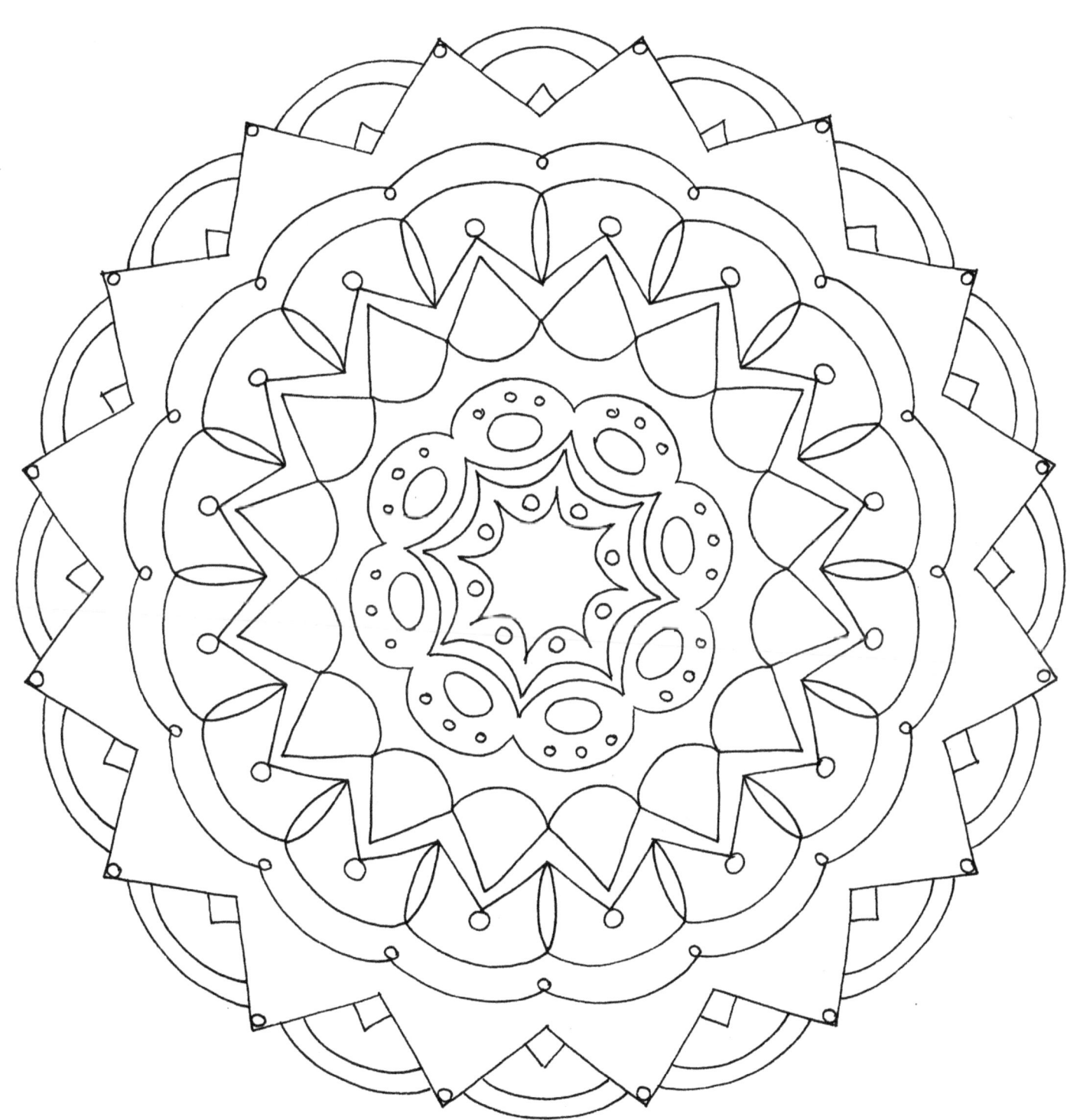

Title:

Date:

Artist:

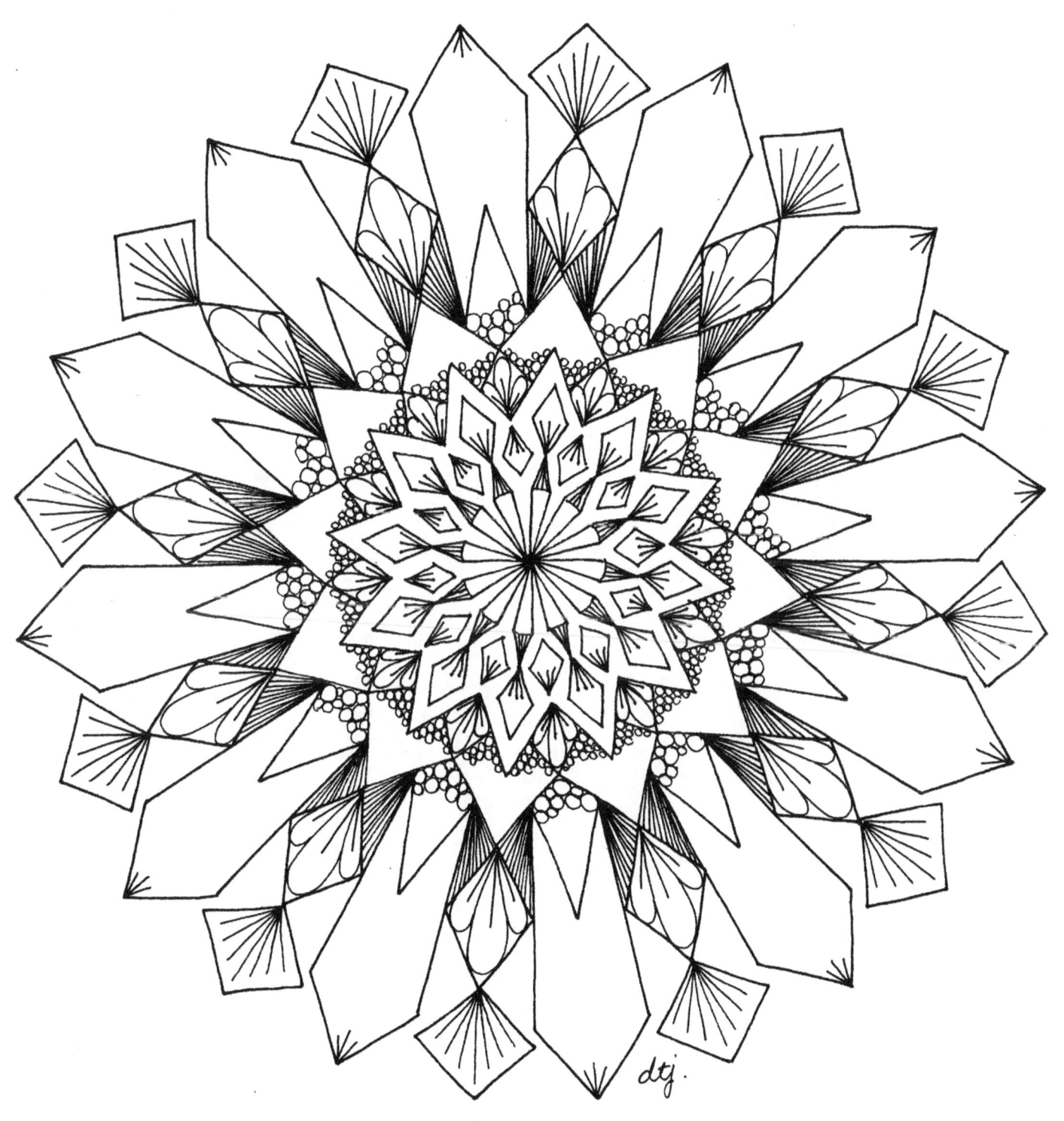

Title:

Date:

Colorist:

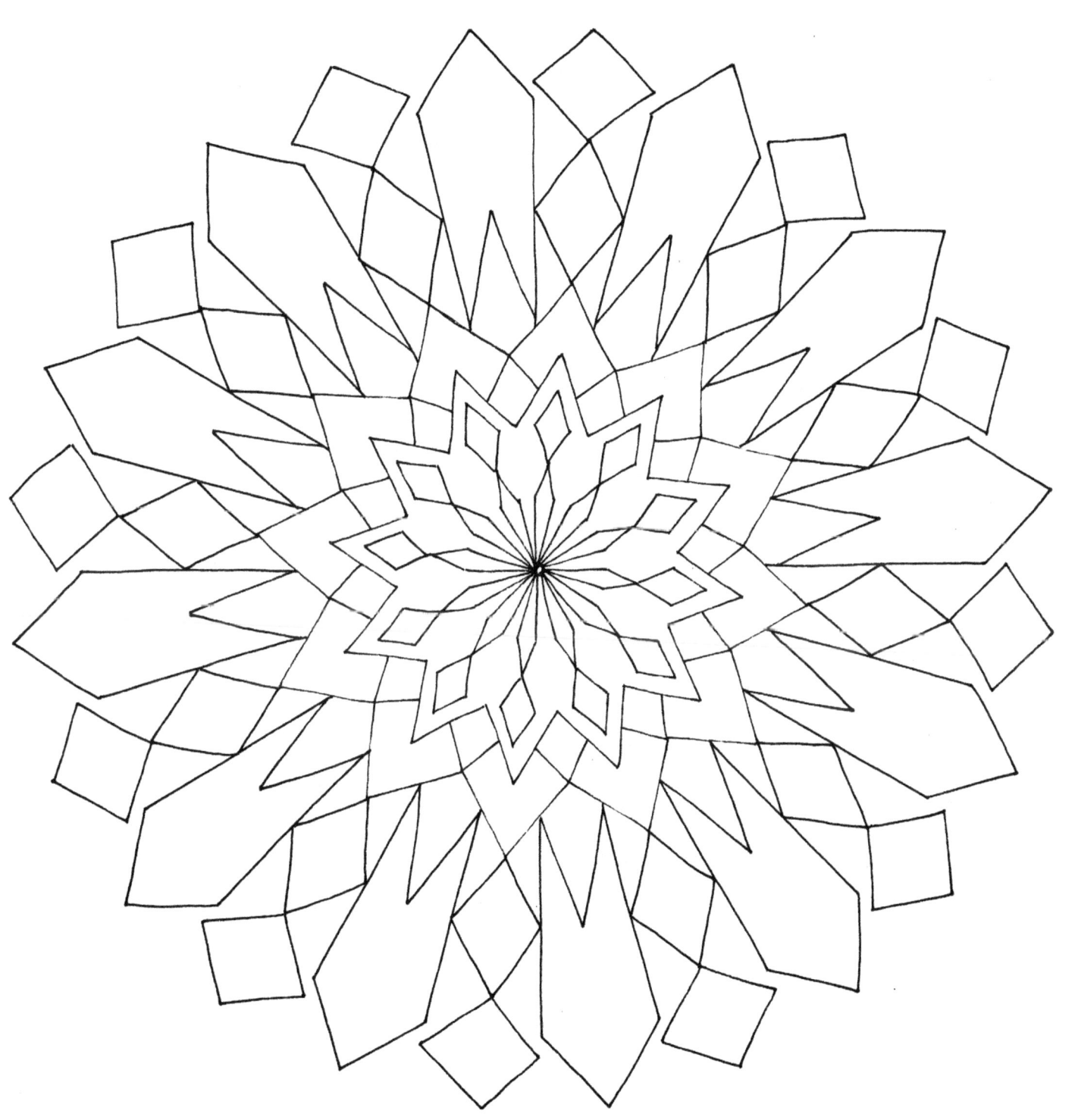

Title:

Date:

Artist:

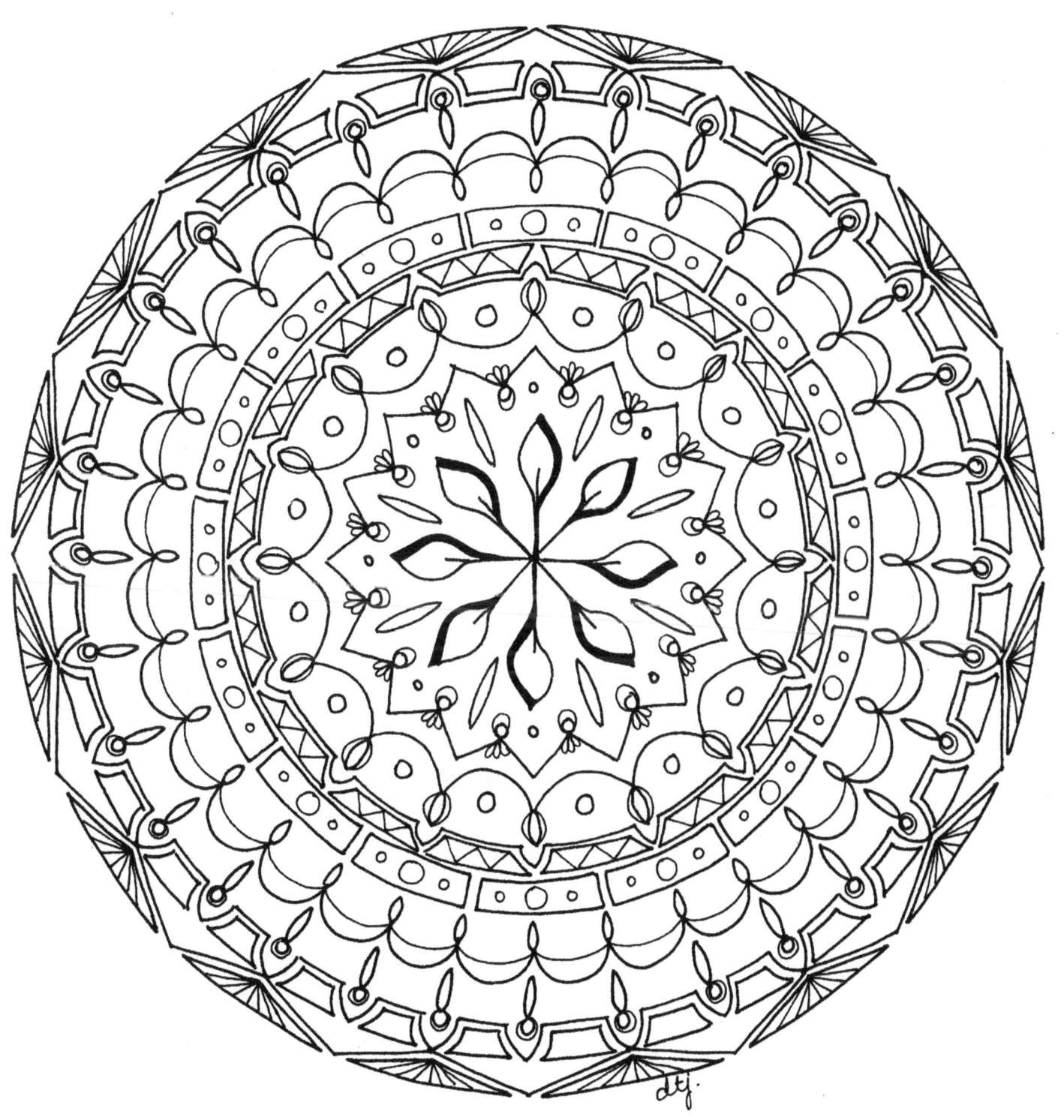

Title:

Date:

Colorist:

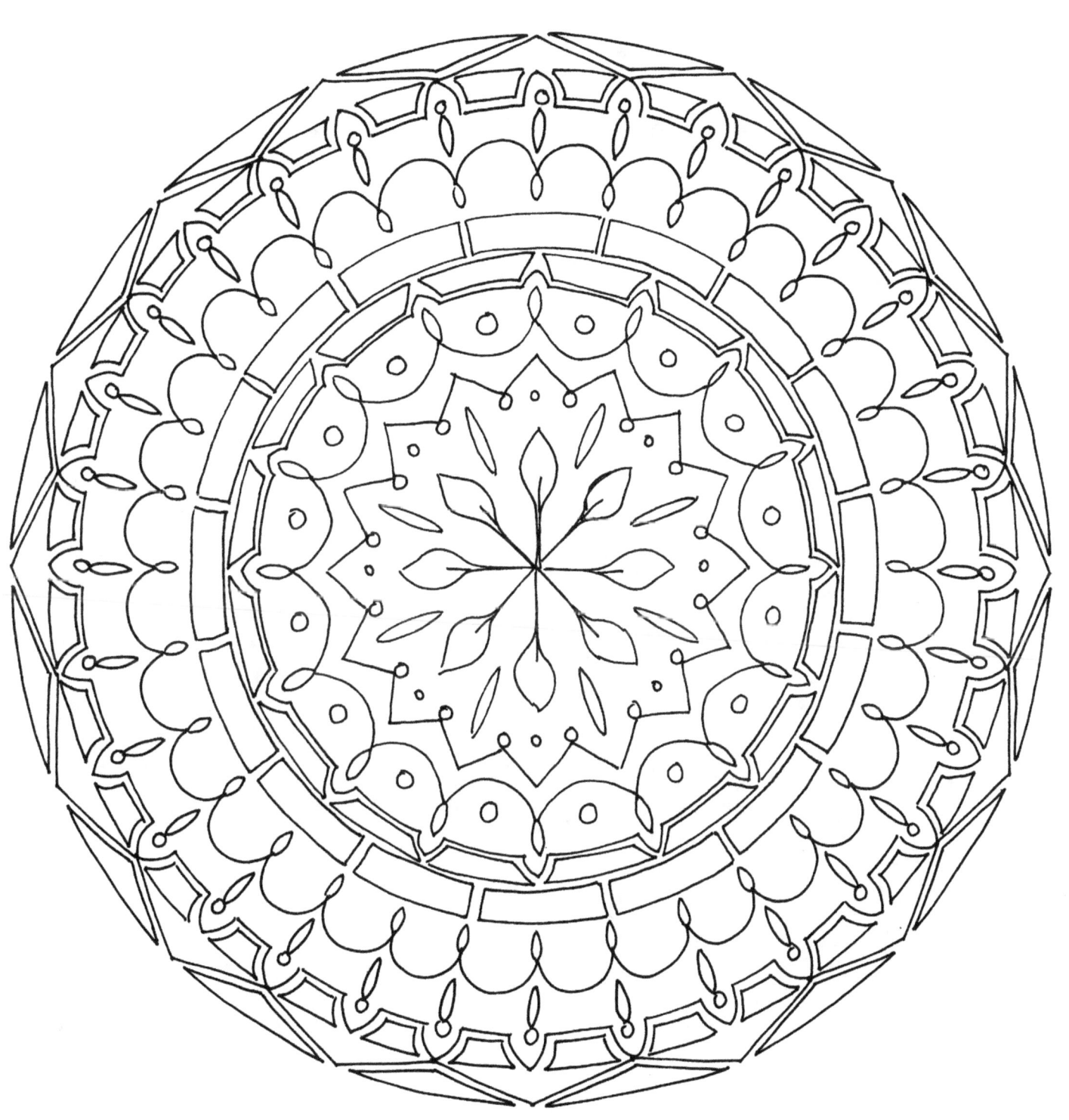

Title:

Date:

Artist:

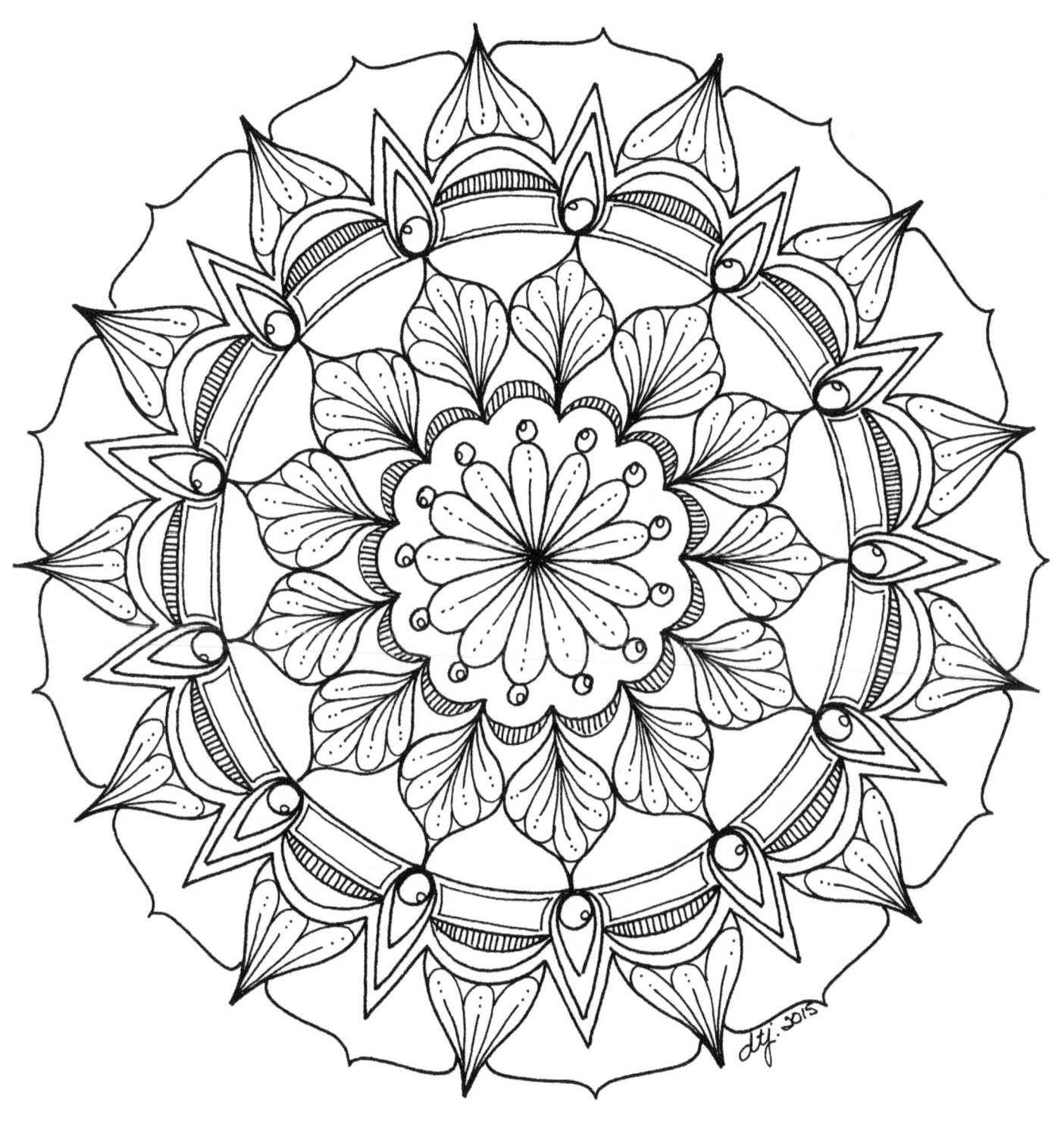

Title:

Date:

Colorist:

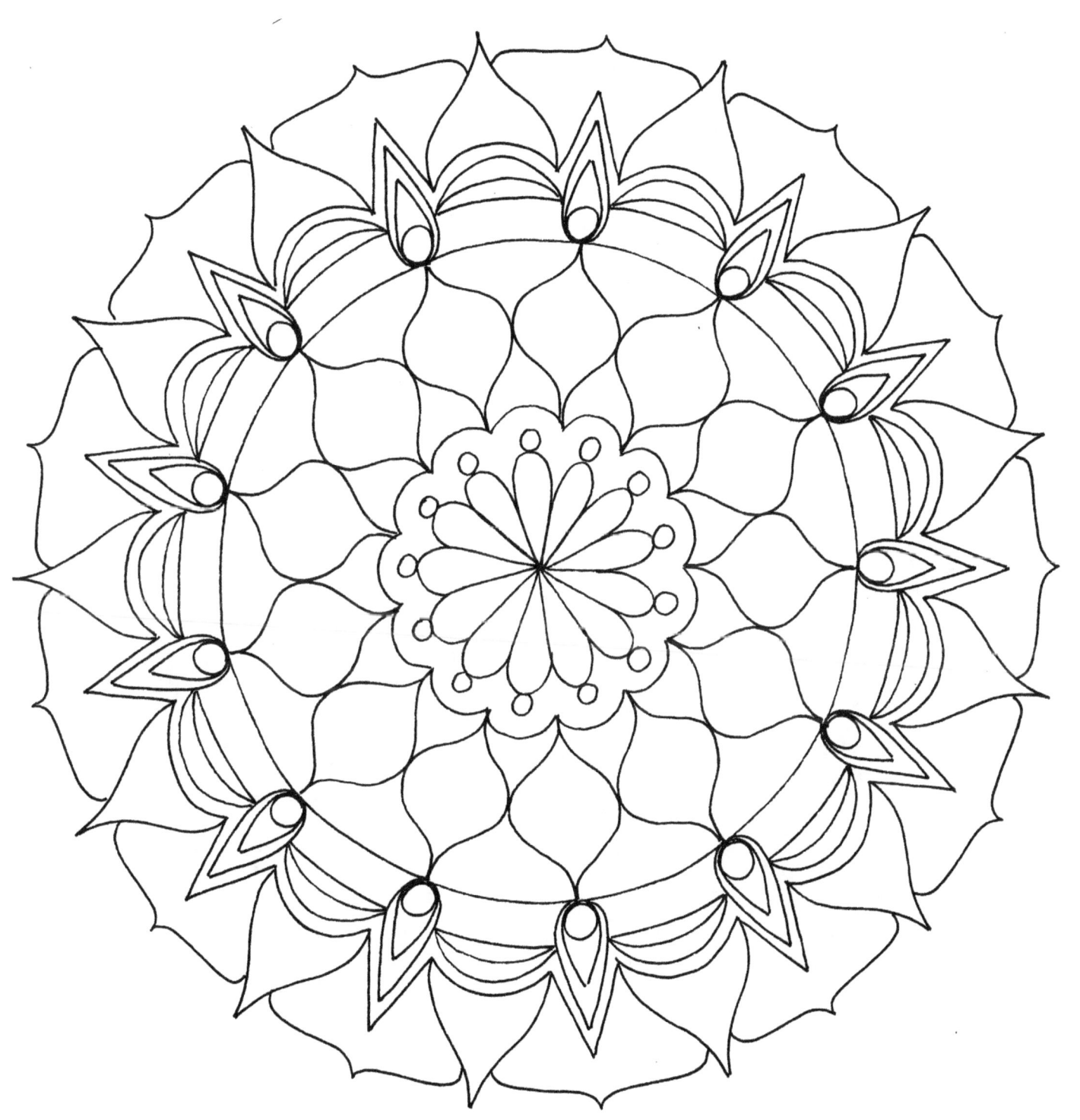

Title:

Date:

Artist:

The following pages have some examples of doodle patterns that you can use for your designs. I have also included some other templates that you can print onto cardstock so that you may design your own Mandalas.

Thank you for purchasing this coloring book and I hope you look forward to the coming coloring/doodle books in the series.

Sincerely,

Darla

Here are 72 doodles that you can use to fill in areas of your own drawings. Patterns are all around us... duplicate the things and patterns that you see around you into your doodles.

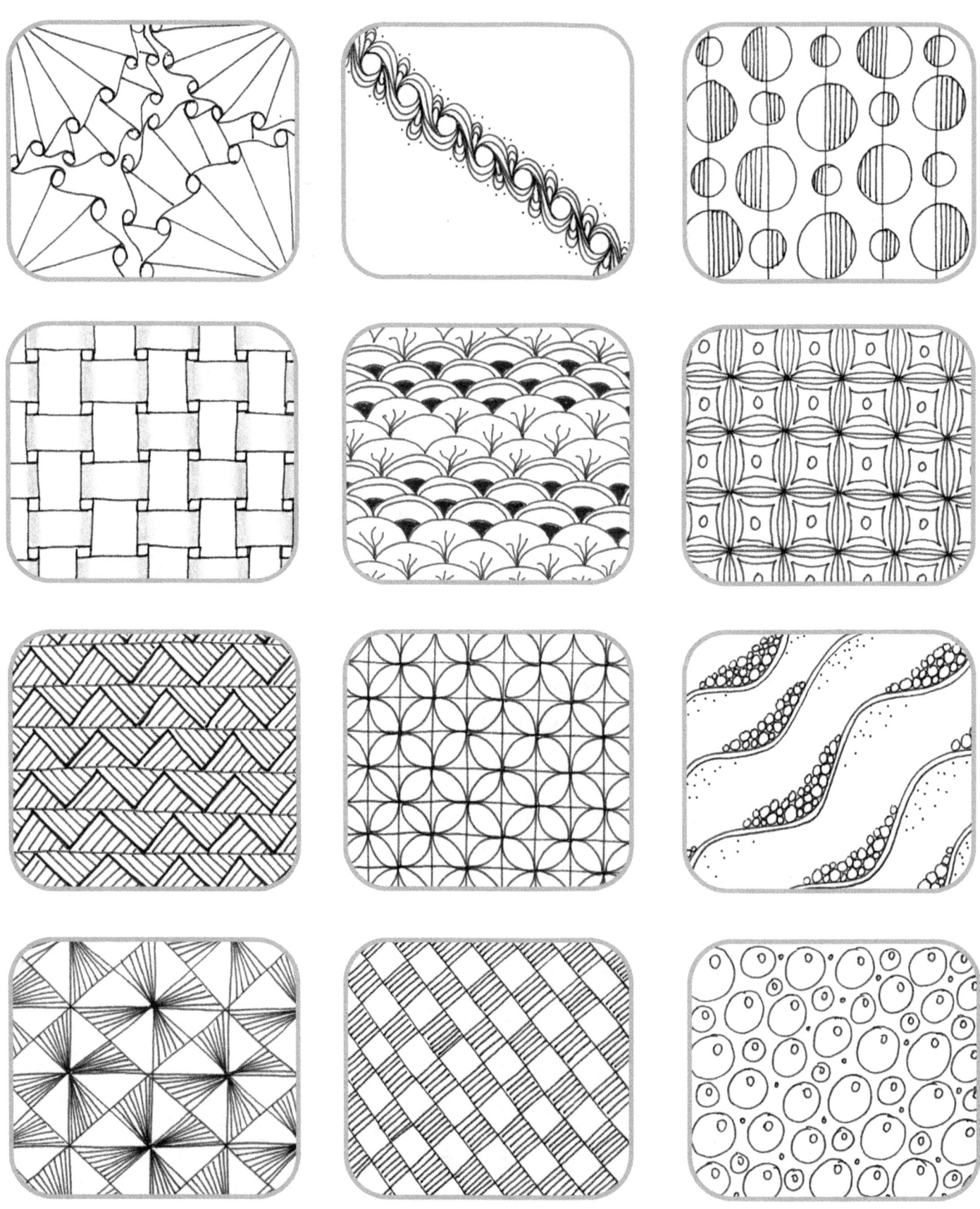

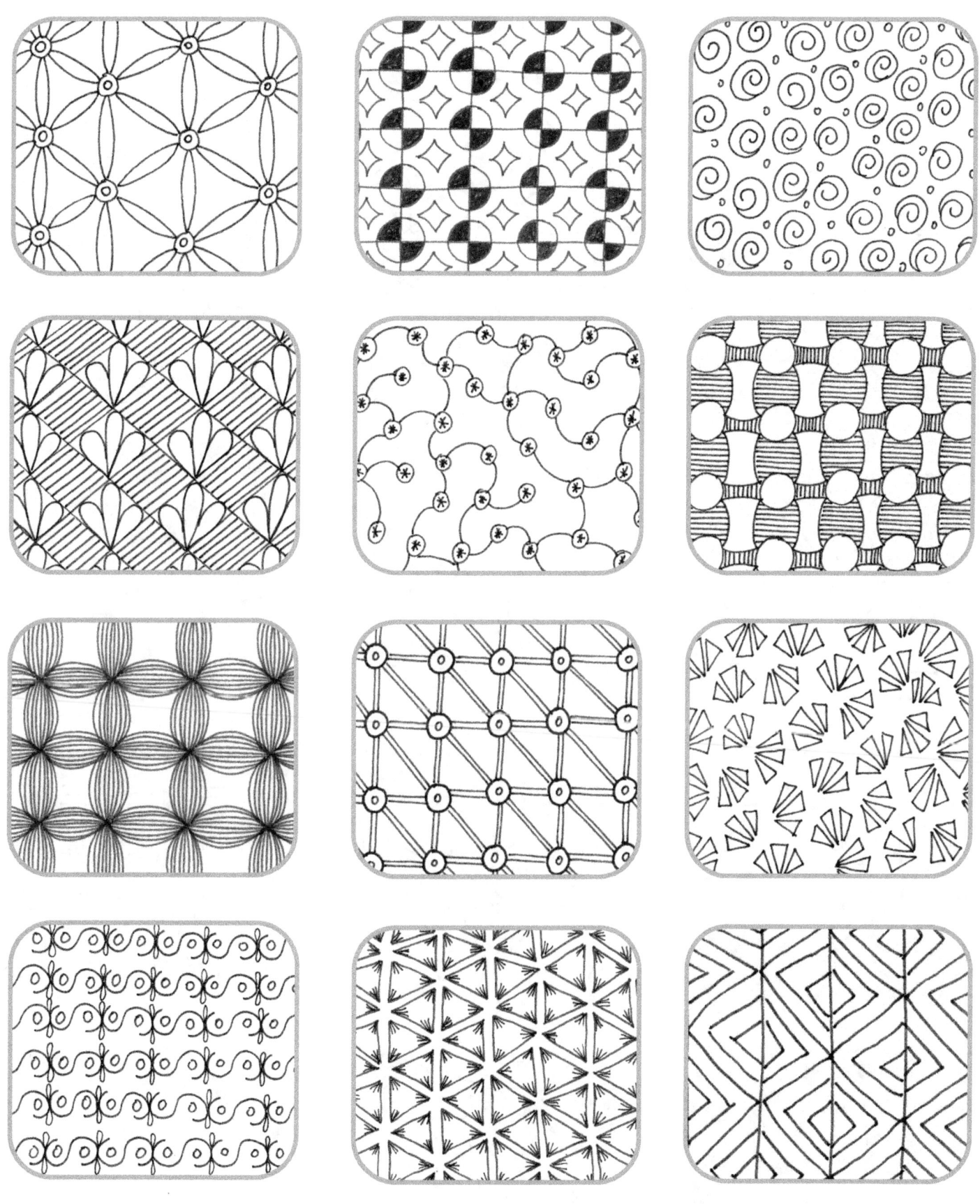

... use your imagination!

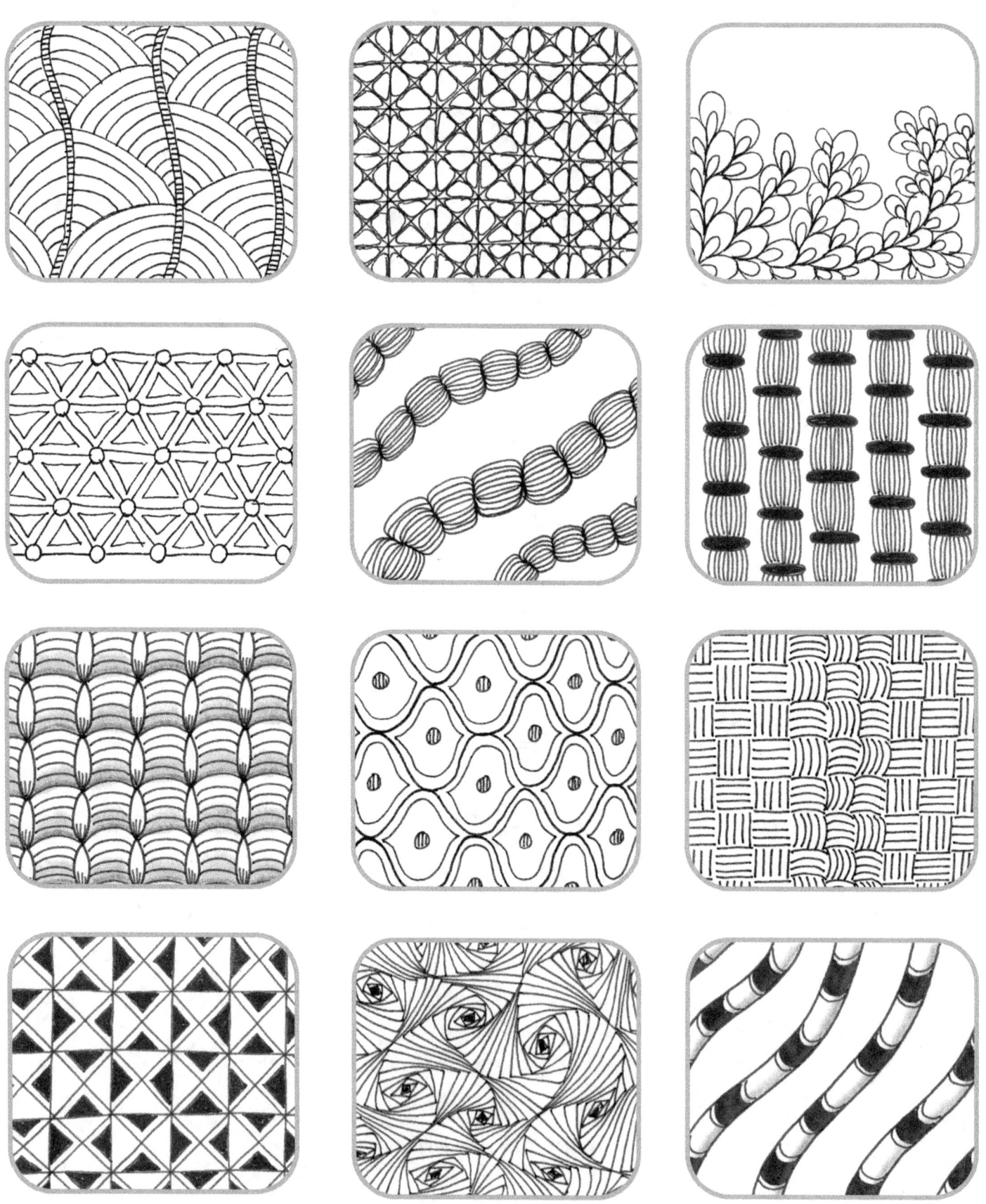

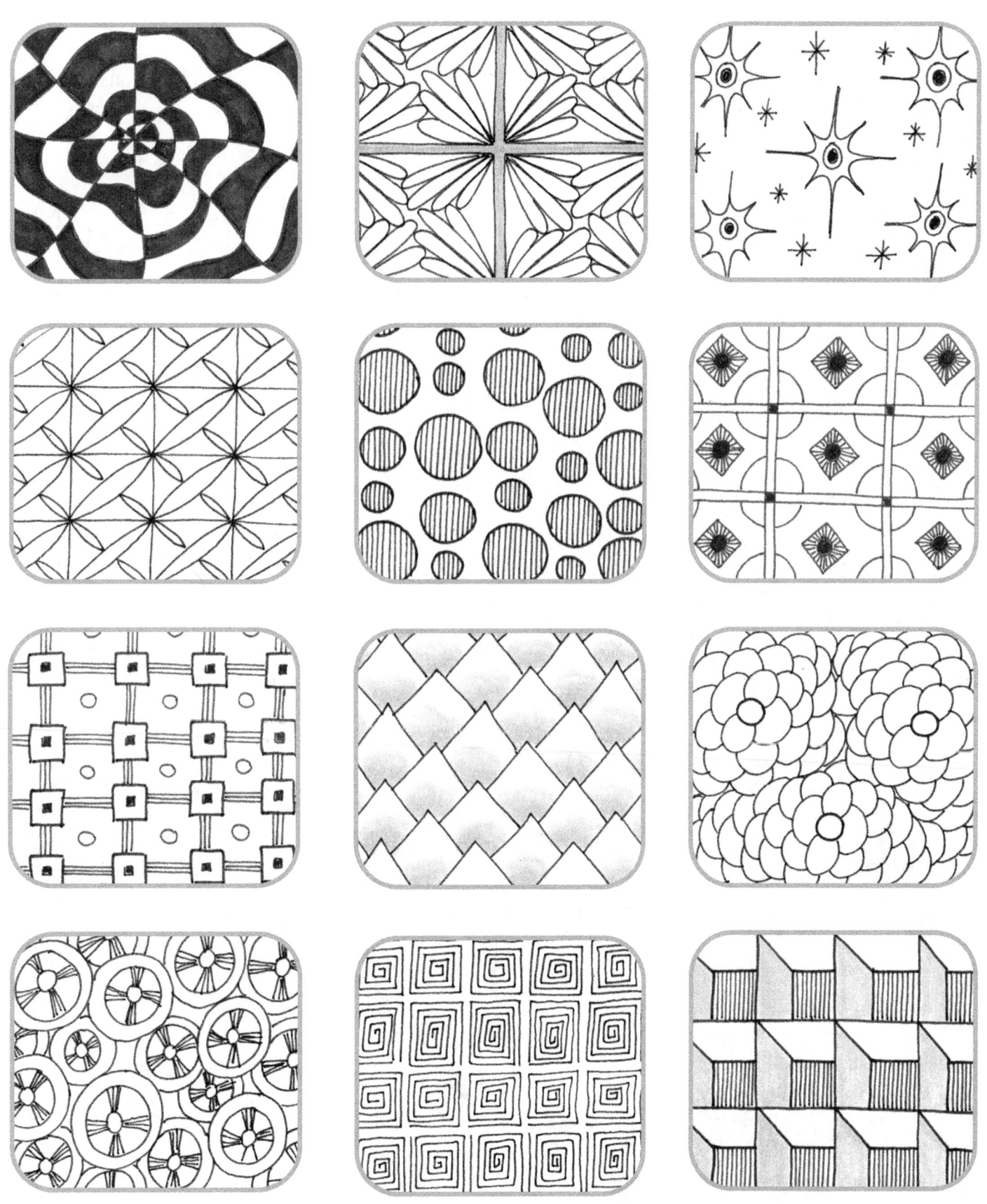

...use shading to add dimension to the doodles.

The last 24 for now.... Shape these to the spaces that you have in your designs.

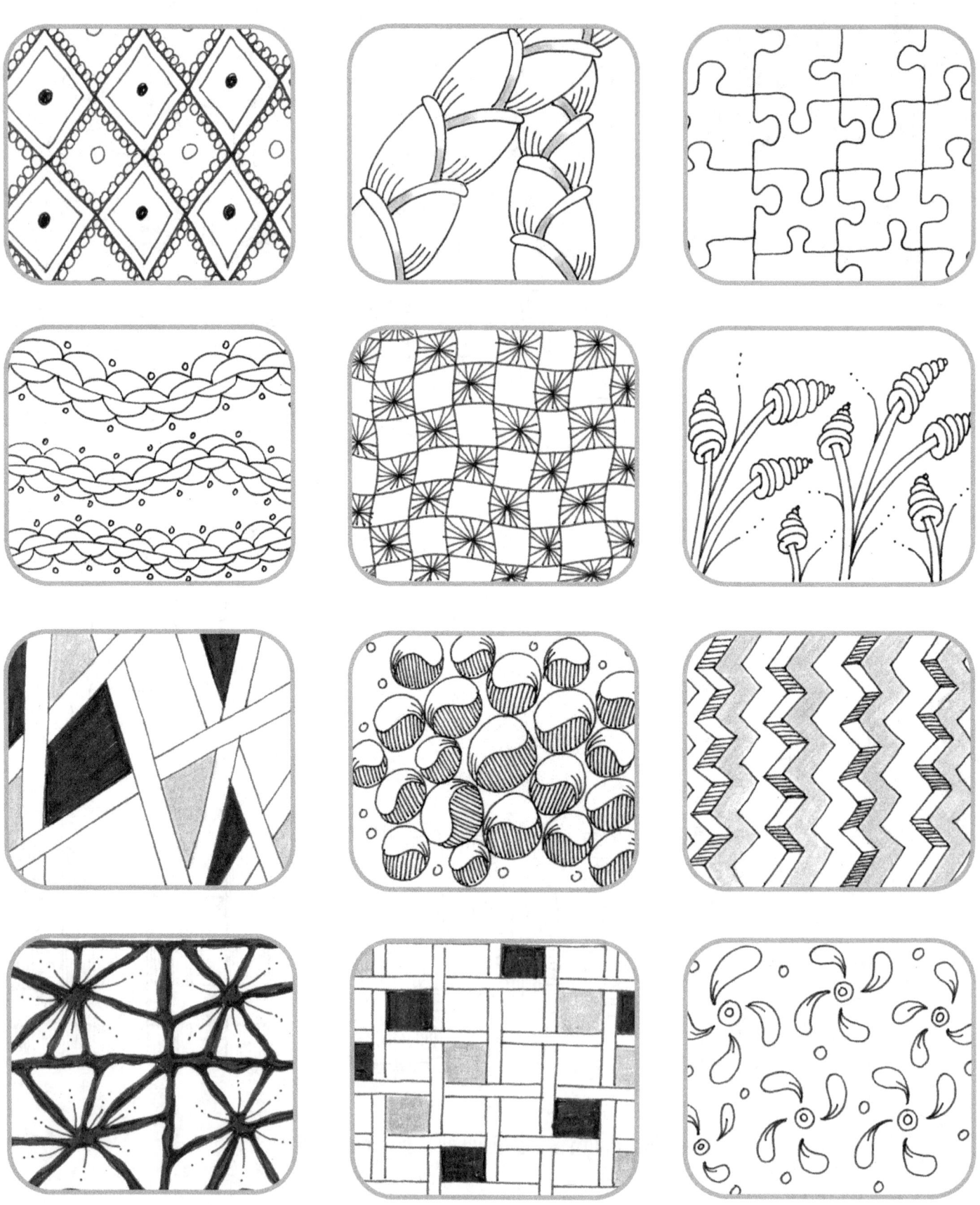

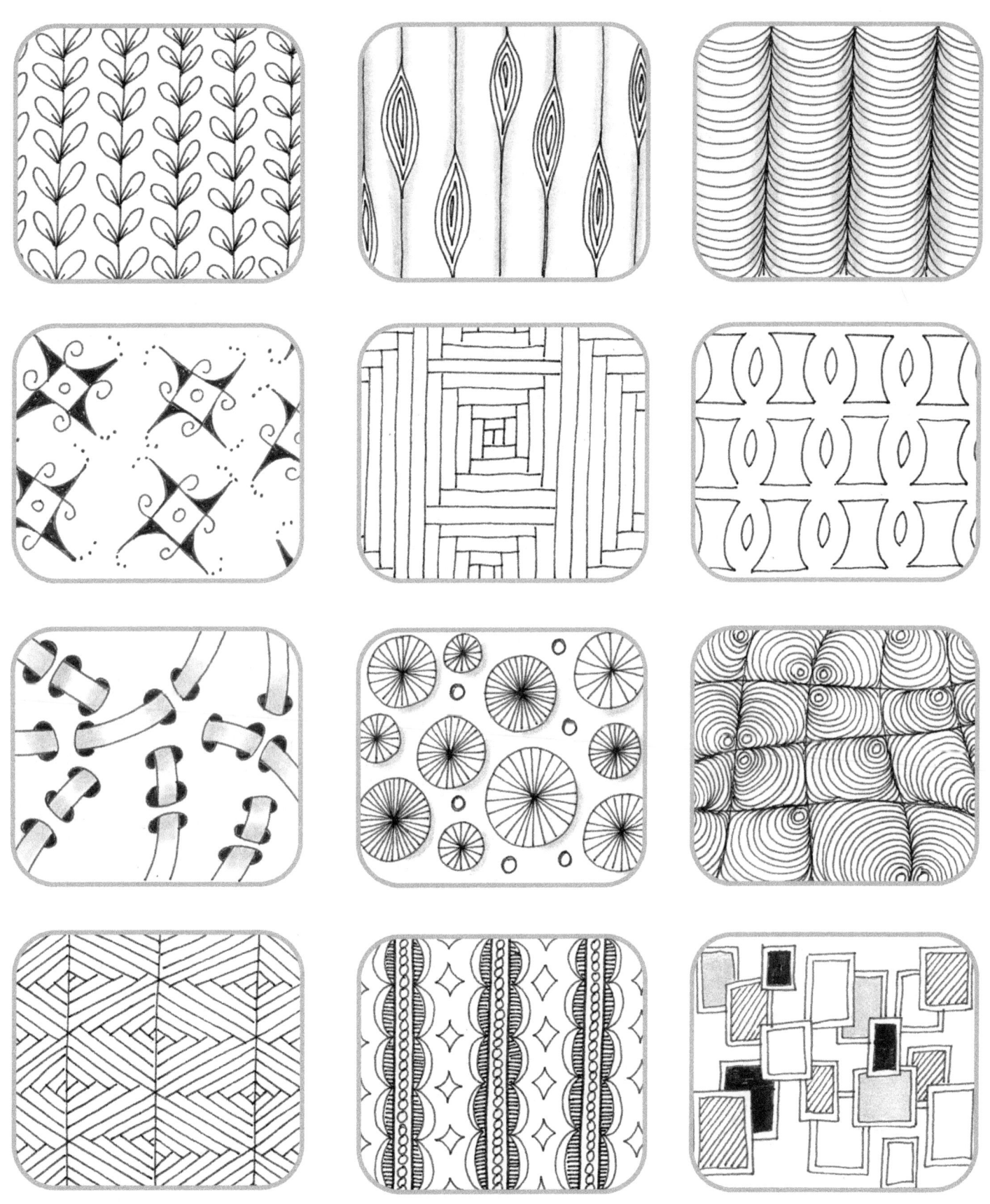

Most importantly, have Fun!!!!

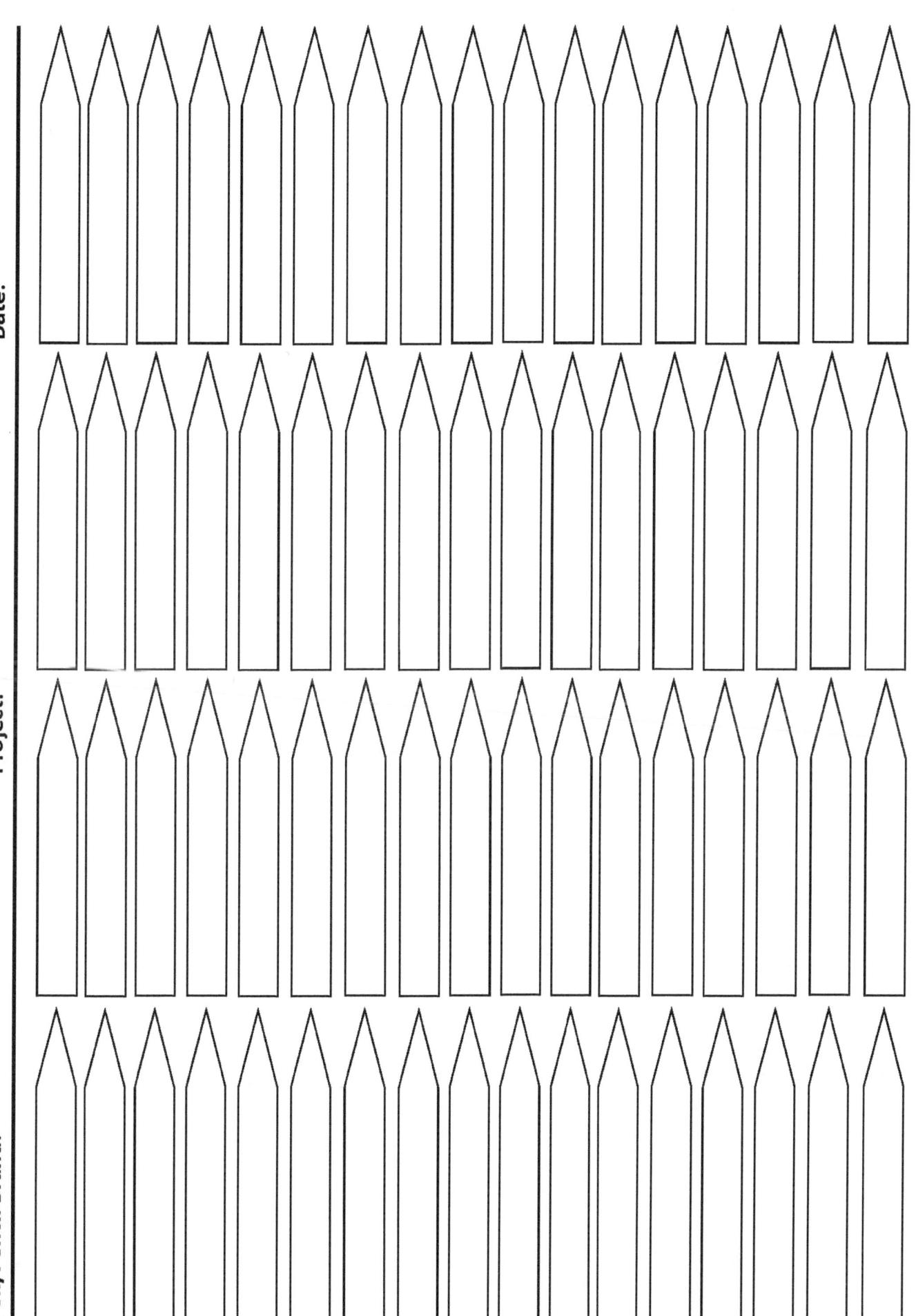

Pen/Pencil Brand:

Project:

Date:

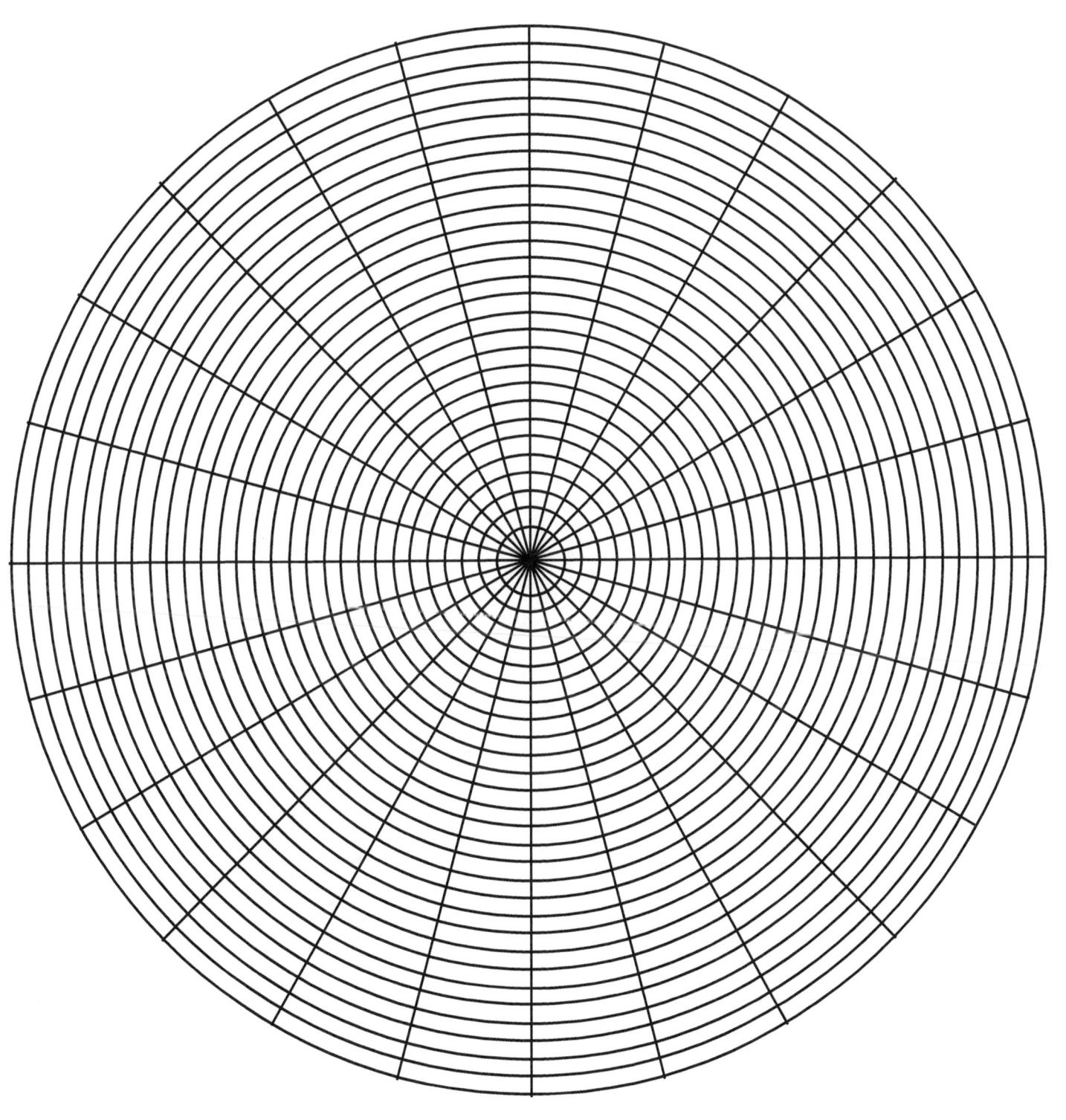

24 Section Reproducible Template for Mandalas

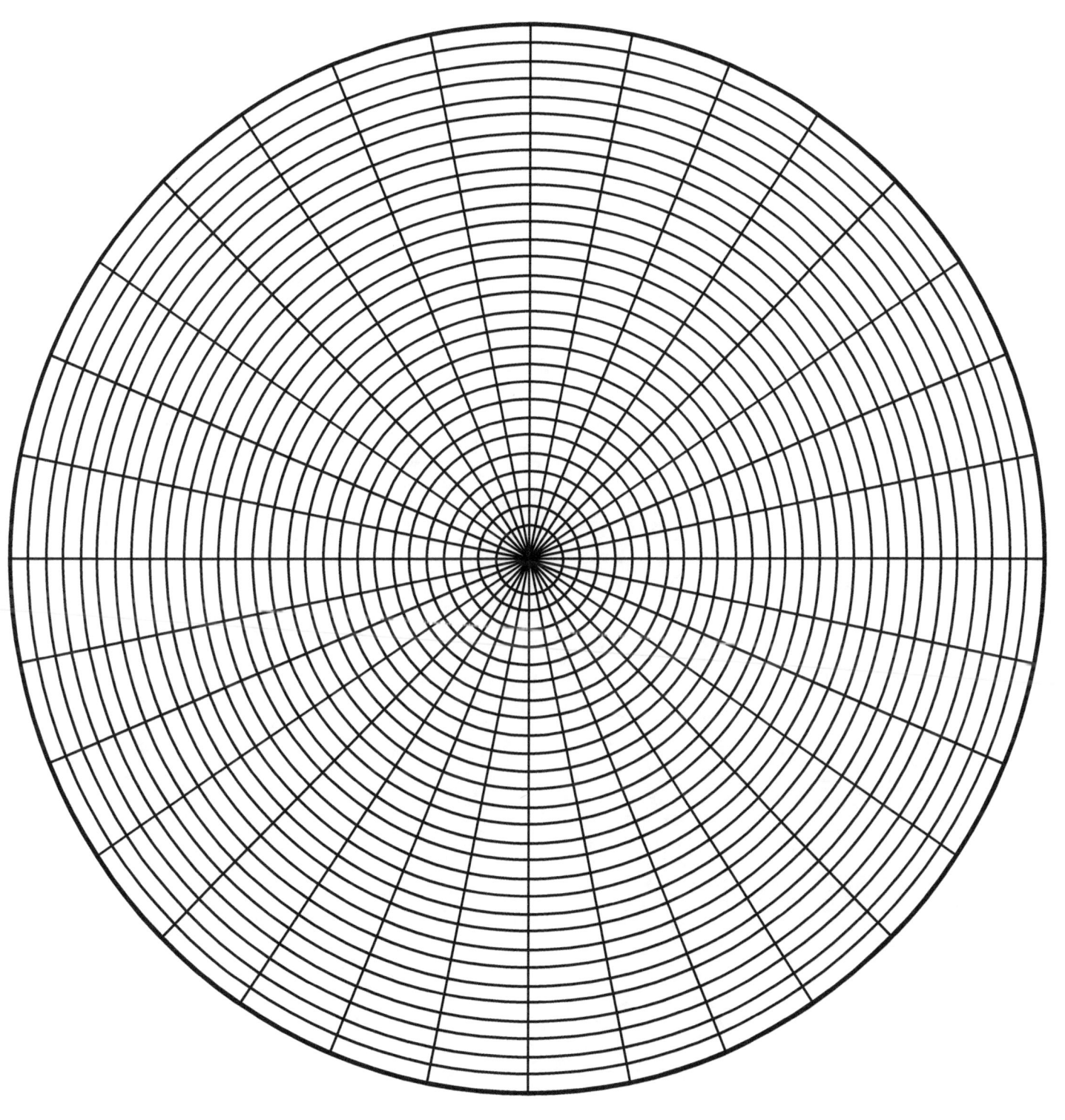

32 Section Reproducible Template for Mandalas